Nathaniel Hawthorne

Passages from the American

Nathaniel Hawthorne

Passages from the American

ISBN/EAN: 9783743355156

Manufactured in Europe, USA, Canada, Australia, Japa

Cover: Foto ©ninafisch / pixelio.de

Manufactured and distributed by brebook publishing software (www.brebook.com)

Nathaniel Hawthorne

Passages from the American

PASSAGES

FROM

NATHANIEL HAWTHORNE'S

AMERICAN NOTE-BOOKS.

PASSAGES

FROM

THE AMERICAN NOTE-BOOKS

OF

NATHANIEL HAWTHORNE,

AUTHOR OF "TRANSFORMATION," "OUR OLD HOME,"
ETC. ETC.

IN TWO VOLUMES.

- VOL. II.

LONDON: SMITH, ELDER AND CO.
1868.

PASSAGES

FROM

HAWTHORNE'S AMERICAN NOTE-BOOKS.

EXTRACTS FROM HIS PRIVATE LETTERS.

BROOK FARM, OAK HILL, *April* 13*th*, 1841.—. . . .
Here I am in a polar Paradise! I know not how to interpret this aspect of nature,—whether it be of good or evil omen to our enterprise. But I reflect that the Plymouth Pilgrims arrived in the midst of storm, and stepped ashore upon mountain snow-drifts; and, nevertheless, they prospered, and became a great people,—and doubtless it will be the same with us. I laud my stars, however, that you will not have your first impressions of (perhaps) our future home from such a day as this. . . . Through faith, I persist in believing that Spring and Summer will come in their due season; but the unregenerated

man shivers within me, and suggests a doubt whether I may not have wandered within the precincts of the Arctic Circle, and chosen my heritage among everlasting snows. . . . Provide yourself with a good stock of furs, and if you can obtain the skin of a polar bear, you will find it a very suitable summer dress for this region. . . .

I have not yet taken my first lesson in agriculture, except that I went to see our cows foddered yesterday afternoon. We have eight of our own; and the number is now increased by a transcendental heifer belonging to Miss Margaret Fuller. She is very fractious, I believe, and apt to kick over the milk-pail. . . . I intend to convert myself into a milkmaid this evening, but I pray Heaven that Mr. Ripley may be moved to assign me the kindliest cow in the herd, otherwise I shall perform my duty with fear and trembling. . . .

I like my brethren in affliction very well; and, could you see us sitting round our table at meal-times, before the great kitchen fire, you would call it a cheerful sight. Mrs. B—— is a most comfortable woman to behold. She looks as if her ample person were stuffed full of tenderness,—indeed, as if she were all one great kind heart. . . .

April 14th, 10 A.M.—. . . . I did not milk the cows last night, because Mr. Ripley was afraid to trust them to my hands, or me to their horns, I know not which. But this morning I have done wonders. Before breakfast, I went out to the barn and began to chop hay for the cattle, and with such "righteous vehemence," as Mr. Ripley says, did I labour, that in the space of ten minutes I broke the machine. Then I brought wood and replenished the fires; and finally went down to breakfast, and ate up a huge mound of buckwheat cakes. After breakfast, Mr. Ripley put a four-pronged instrument into my hands, which he gave me to understand was called a pitchfork; and he and Mr. Farley being armed with similar weapons, we all three commenced a gallant attack upon a heap of manure. This office being concluded, and I having purified myself, I sit down to finish this letter. . . .

Miss Fuller's cow hooks the other cows, and has made herself ruler of the herd, and behaves in a very tyrannical manner. . . . I shall make an excellent husbandman,—I feel the original Adam reviving within me.

April 16th.—. . . . Since I last wrote, there has been an addition to our community of four gentlemen in sables, who promise to be among our most useful and respectable members. They arrived yesterday, about noon. Mr. Ripley had proposed to them to join us, no longer ago than that very morning. I had some conversation with them in the afternoon, and was glad to hear them express much satisfaction with their new abode and all the arrangements. They do not appear to be very communicative, however,—or perhaps it may be merely an external reserve, like my own, to shield their delicacy. Several of their prominent characteristics, as well as their black attire, lead me to believe that they are members of the clerical profession; but I have not yet ascertained from their own lips what has been the nature of their past lives. I trust to have much pleasure in their society, and, sooner or later, that we shall all of us derive great strength from our intercourse with them. I cannot too highly applaud the readiness with which these four gentlemen in black have thrown aside all the fopperies and flummeries which have their origin in a false state of society. When I last saw them, they looked as heroically regardless of the stains and soils incident to our profession as I did when I emerged from the gold-mine. . . .

I have milked a cow!!! ... The herd has rebelled against the usurpation of Miss Fuller's heifer; and, whenever they are turned out of the barn, she is compelled to take refuge under our protection. So much did she impede my labours by keeping close to me, that I found it necessary to give her two or three gentle pats with a shovel; but still she preferred to trust herself to my tender mercies, rather than venture among the horns of the herd. She is not an amiable cow; but she has a very intelligent face, and seems to be of a reflective cast of character. I doubt not that she will soon perceive the expediency of being on good terms with the rest of the sisterhood.

I have not yet been twenty yards from our house and barn; but I begin to perceive that this is a beautiful place. The scenery is of a mild and placid character, with nothing bold in its aspect; but I think its beauties will grow upon us, and make us love it the more the longer we live here. There is a brook, so near the house that we shall be able to hear its ripple in the summer evenings, ... but, for agricultural purposes, it has been made to flow in a straight and rectangular fashion, which does it infinite damage as a picturesque object. ...

It was a moment or two before I could think

ing a grindstone all the forenoon; and such occupations are apt to disturb the equilibrium of the muscles and sinews. It is an endless surprise to me how much work there is to be done in the world; but, thank God, I am able to do my share of it,—and my ability increases daily. What a great, broad-shouldered, elephantine personage I shall become by and by!

* * * * *

I milked two cows this morning, and would send you some of the milk, only that it is mingled with that which was drawn forth by Mr. Dismal View and the rest of the brethren.

April 28*th.*— . . . I was caught by a cold during my visit to Boston. It has not affected my whole frame, but took entire possession of my head, as being the weakest and most vulnerable part. Never did anybody sneeze with such vehemence and frequency; and my poor brain has been in a thick fog, or, rather, it seemed as if my head were stuffed with coarse wool. . . . Sometimes I wanted to wrench it off, and give it a great kick, like a football.

This annoyance has made me endure the bad weather with even less than ordinary patience; and my faith was so far exhausted that, when they told me yesterday that the sun was setting clear, I would not even turn my eyes towards the west. But this morning I am made all over anew, and have no greater remnant of my cold than will serve as an excuse for doing no work to-day.

* * * * *

The family has been dismal and dolorous throughout the storm. The night before last, William Allen was stung by a wasp on the eyelid; whereupon the whole side of his face swelled to an enormous magnitude, so that, at the breakfast-table, one half of him looked like a blind giant (the eye being closed), and the other half had such a sorrowful and ludicrous aspect that I was constrained to laugh out of sheer pity. The same day a colony of wasps was discovered in my chamber, where they had remained throughout the winter, and were now just bestirring themselves, doubtless with the intention of stinging me from head to foot. . . . A similar discovery was made in Mr. Farley's room. In short, we seem to have taken up our abode in a wasps' nest. Thus you see a rural life is not one of unbroken quiet and serenity.

If the middle of the day prove warm and pleasant, I promise myself to take a walk. . . . I have taken one walk with Mr. Farley: and I could not have believed that there was such seclusion at so short a distance from a great city. Many spots seem hardly to have been visited for ages,—not since John Eliot preached to the Indians here. If we were to travel a thousand miles, we could not escape the world more completely than we can here.

* * * * *

I read no newspapers, and hardly remember who is President, and feel as if I had no more concern with what other people trouble themselves about than if I dwelt in another planet.

May 1st.— ... Every day of my life makes me feel more and more how seldom a fact is accurately stated; how, almost invariably, when a story has passed through the mind of a third person, it becomes, so far as regards the impression that it makes in further repetitions, little better than a falsehood, and this, too, though the narrator be the most truth-seeking person in existence. How marvellous the tendency is. ... Is truth a fantasy which we are to pursue for ever, and never grasp?

* * * * *

My cold has almost entirely departed. Were it a

sunny day, I should consider myself quite fit for labour out of doors; but as the ground is so damp, and the atmosphere so chill, and the sky so sullen, I intend to keep myself on the sick list this one day longer, more especially as I wish to read Carlyle on Heroes.

*　　　*　　　*　　　*　　　*

There has been but one flower found in this vicinity,—and that was an anemone, a poor, pale, shivering little flower, that had crept under a stone wall for shelter. Mr. Farley found it, while taking a walk with me.

. . . . This is May-day! Alas, what a difference between the ideal and the real!

May 4th.—. . . . . My cold no longer troubles me, and all the morning I have been at work under the clear blue sky, on a hill-side. Sometimes it almost seemed as if I were at work in the sky itself, though the material in which I wrought was the ore from our gold-mine. Nevertheless, there is nothing so unseemly and disagreeable in this sort of toil as you could think. It defiles the hands, indeed, but not the soul. This gold ore is a pure and wholesome substance, else our mother Nature would not devour it so readily, and derive so much nourishment from it, and return such a rich abundance of good grain and roots in requital of it.

The farm is growing very beautiful now,—not that we yet see anything of the peas and potatoes which we have planted; but the grass blushes green on the slopes and hollows. I wrote that word "blush" almost unconsciously; so we will let it go as an inspired utterance. When I go forth afield, ... I look beneath the stone walls where the verdure is richest, in hopes that a little company of violets, or some solitary bud, prophetic of the summer, may be there .... but not a wild-flower have I yet found. One of the boys gathered some yellow cowslips last Sunday; but I am well content not to have found them, for they are not precisely what I should like to send to you, though they deserve honour and praise, because they come to us when no others will. We have our parlour here dressed in evergreen, as at Christmas. That beautiful little flower vase .... stands on Mr. Ripley's study table, at which I am now writing. It contains some daffodils and some willow blossoms. I brought it here rather than keep it in my chamber, because I never sit there, and it gives me many pleasant emotions to look round and be surprised—for it is often a surprise, though I well know that it is there—by something connected with the idea [of a friend].

* * * * *

I do not believe that I should be patient here if I were not engaged in a righteous and heaven-blessed way of life. When I was in the Custom House, and then at Salem, I was not half so patient. . . .

We had some tableaux last evening, the principal characters being sustained by Mr. Farley and Miss Ellen Slade. They went off very well. . . .

I fear it is time for me—sod-compelling as I am—to take the field again.

May 11*th.*—. . . . This morning I arose at milking-time in good trim for work; and we have been employed partly in an Augean labour of clearing out a wood-shed, and partly in carting loads of oak. This afternoon I hope to have something to do in the field, for these jobs about the house are not at all to my taste.

June 1*st.*—. . . . I have been too busy to write a long letter by this opportunity, for I think this present life of mine gives me an antipathy to pen and ink,

even more than my Custom House experience did.
. . . . In the midst of toil, or after a hard day's work
in the gold-mine, my soul obstinately refuses to be
poured out on paper. That abominable gold-mine!
Thank God, we anticipate getting rid of its treasures
in the course of two or three days! Of all hateful
places that is the worst, and I shall never comfort
myself for having spent so many days of blessed
sunshine there. It is my opinion that a man's soul
may be buried and perish under a dung-heap, or in
a furrow of the field, just as well as under a pile of
money.

Mr. George Bradford will probably be here to-day,
so that there will be no danger of my being under the
necessity of labouring more than I like hereafter.
Meantime my health is perfect, and my spirits buoy-
ant, even in the gold-mine.

August 12*th.*—. . . . I am very well, and not at
all weary, for yesterday's rain gave us a holiday; and
moreover, the labours of the farm are not so pressing
as they have been. And, joyful thought! in a little
more than a fortnight I shall be free from my bondage,—. . . . free to enjoy Nature,—free to think and
feel! . . . . Even my Custom House experience was

not such a thraldom and weariness; my mind and heart were free. Oh, labour is the curse of the world, and nobody can meddle with it without becoming proportionably brutified! Is it a praiseworthy matter that I have spent five golden months in providing food for cows and horses? It is not so.

August 18*th.*—I am very well, only somewhat tired with walking half-a-dozen miles immediately after breakfast, and raking hay ever since. We shall quite finish haying this week, and then there will be no more very hard or constant labour during the one other week that I shall remain a slave.

August 22*nd.*—. . . . I had an indispensable engagement in the bean-field, whither, indeed, I was glad to betake myself, in order to escape a parting scene with ——. He was quite out of his wits the night before, and I sat up with him till long past midnight. The farm is pleasanter now that he is gone; for his unappeasable wretchedness threw a gloom over everything. Since I last wrote, we have done haying, and the remainder of my bondage will probably be light. It will be a long time, however, before I shall know how to make a good use of leisure, either as regards enjoyment or literary occupation. . . .

It is extremely doubtful whether Mr. Ripley will succeed in locating his community on this farm. He can bring Mr. E—— to no terms, and the more they talk about the matter, the further they appear to be from a settlement. We must form other plans for ourselves; for I can see few or no signs that Providence purposes to give us a home here. I am weary, weary, thrice weary, of waiting so many ages. Whatever may be my gifts, I have not hitherto shown a single one that may avail to gather gold. I confess that I have strong hopes of good from this arrangement with M——; but when I look at the scanty avails of my past literary efforts, I do not feel authorized to expect much from the future. Well, we shall see. Other persons have bought large estates and built splendid mansions with such little books as I mean to write; so that perhaps it is not unreasonable to hope that mine may enable me to build a little cottage, or, at least, to buy or hire one. But I am becoming more and more convinced that we must not lean upon this community. Whatever is to be done must be done by my own undivided strength. I shall not remain here through the winter, unless with an absolute certainty that there will be a house ready for us in the spring. Otherwise, I shall return to Boston;— still, however, considering myself an associate of the community, so that we may take advantage of any more favourable aspect of affairs. How much depends on these little books! Methinks if anything could draw out my whole strength, it would be the motives that now press upon me. Yet, after all, I must keep these considerations out of my mind, because an external pressure always disturbs instead of assisting me.

Salem, September 3rd.—. . . . But really I should judge it to be twenty years since I left Brook Farm; and I take this to be one proof that my life there was an unnatural and unsuitable, and therefore an unreal one. It already looks like a dream behind me. The real Me was never an associate of the community; there has been a spectral Appearance there, sounding the horn at daybreak, and milking the cows, and hoeing potatoes, and raking hay, toiling in the sun, and doing me the honour to assume my name. But this spectre was not myself. Nevertheless, it is somewhat remarkable that my hands have, during the past summer, grown very brown and rough, insomuch that many people persist in believing that I, after all, was the aforesaid spectral horn-sounder, cow-milker, potato-hoer, and hay-raker. But such people do not know a reality from a shadow. Enough of nonsense. I know not exactly how soon I shall return to the farm. Perhaps not sooner than a fortnight from to-morrow.

Salem, September 14*th.*— .... Master Cheever is a very good subject for a sketch, especially if he be portrayed in the very act of executing judgment on an evil-doer. The little urchin may be laid across his knee, and his arms and legs, and whole person indeed, should be flying all abroad, in an agony of nervous excitement and corporeal smart. The Master, on the other hand, must be calm, rigid, without anger or pity, the very personification of that immitigable law whereby suffering follows sin. Meantime the lion's head should have a sort of sly twist on one side of its mouth, and a wink of one eye, in order to give the impression that, after all, the crime and the punishment are neither of them the most serious things in the world. I could draw the sketch myself, if I had but the use of ——'s magic fingers.

Then the Acadians will do very well for the second sketch. They might be represented as just landing on the wharf; or as presenting themselves before Governor Shirley, seated in the great chair. Another subject might be old Cotton Mather, venerable in a three-cornered hat and other antique attire, walking the streets of Boston, and lifting up his hands to bless the people, while they all revile him. An old dame should be seen, flinging water, or emptying some vials of medicine on his head from the latticed window of an old-fashioned house; and all around must be tokens of pestilence and mourning,—as a coffin borne along,—a woman or children weeping on a doorstep. Can the tolling of the Old South bell be painted?

If not this, then the military council holden at Boston by the Earl of Loudon and other captains and governors, might be taken,—his lordship in the great chair, an old-fashioned, military figure, with a star on his breast. Some of Louis XV.'s commanders will give the costume. On the table, and scattered about the room, must be symbols of warfare,— swords, pistols, plumed hats, a drum, trumpet, and rolled-up banner in one heap. It were not amiss to introduce the armed figure of an Indian chief, as taking part in the council,—or standing apart from the English, erect and stern.

Now for Liberty Tree. There is an engraving of that famous vegetable in Snow's *History of Boston*. If represented, I see not what scene can be beneath it, save poor Mr. Oliver, taking the oath. He must have on a bag-wig, ruffled sleeves, embroidered coat, and all such ornaments, because he is the representative of aristocracy and an artificial system. The people may be as rough and wild as the fancy can make them; nevertheless, there must be one or two grave, puritanical figures in the midst. Such an one might sit in the great chair, and be an emblem of that stern, considerate spirit which brought about the Revolution. But this would be a hard subject.

But what a dolt am I to obtrude my counsel. . . .

September 16th.— . . . . I do not very well recollect Monsieur du Miroir, but, as to Mrs. Bullfrog, I give her up to the severest reprehension. The story was written as a mere experiment in that style; it did not come from any depth within me,—neither my heart nor mind had anything to do with it. I recollect that the Man of Adamant seemed a fine idea to me when I looked at it prophetically; but I failed in giving shape and substance to the vision which I saw. I don't think it can be very good. . .

I cannot believe all these stories about ———, because such a rascal never could be sustained and countenanced by respectable men. I take him to be neither better nor worse than the average of his tribe. However, I intend to have all my copyrights taken out in my own name; and, if he cheat me once, I will have nothing more to do with him, but will straightway be cheated by some other publisher,—that being, of course, the only alternative.

* * * * *

Governor Shirley's young French wife might be the subject of one of the cuts. She should sit in the great chair,—perhaps with a dressing-glass before her,—and arrayed in all manner of fantastic finery, and with an *outré* French air, while the old Governor is leaning fondly over her, and a puritanic counsellor or two are manifesting their disgust in the background. A negro footman and a French waiting-maid might be in attendance.

* * * * *

In Liberty Tree might be a vignette, representing the chair in a very shattered, battered, and forlorn condition, after it had been ejected from Hutchinson's house. This would serve to impress the reader with the woeful vicissitudes of sublunary things. . . .

Did you ever behold such a vile scribble as I write since I became a farmer? My chirography always was abominable, but now it is outrageous.

Brook Farm, September 22nd, 1841.— . . . . Here I am again, slowly adapting myself to the life of this queer community, whence I seem to have been absent half a lifetime,—so utterly have I grown apart from the spirit and manners of the place. . . . . I was most kindly received; and the fields and woods looked very pleasant in the bright sunshine of the day before yesterday. I had a friendlier disposition towards the farm, now that I am no longer obliged to toil in its stubborn furrows. Yesterday and to-day, however, the weather has been intolerable,—cold, chill, sullen, so that it is impossible to be on kindly terms with Mother Nature. . . . .

I doubt whether I shall succeed in writing another volume of Grandfather's Library while I remain here. I have not the sense of perfect seclusion which has always been essential to my power of producing anything. It is true, nobody intrudes into my room; but still I cannot be quiet. Nothing here is settled; everything is but beginning to arrange itself, and though I would seem to have little to do with aught beside my own thoughts, still I cannot but partake of the ferment around me. My mind will not be abstracted. I must observe, and think, and feel, and content myself with catching glimpses of things which may be wrought out hereafter. Perhaps it will be quite as well that I find myself unable to set seriously about literary occupation for the present. It will be good to have a longer interval between my labour of the body and that of the mind. I shall work to the better purpose after the beginning of November. Meantime I shall see these people and their enterprise under a new point of view, and perhaps be able to determine whether we have any call to cast in our lot among them.

* * * * *

I do wish the weather would put off this sulky mood. Had it not been for the warmth and brightness of Monday, when I arrived here, I should have supposed that all sunshine had left Brook Farm for ever. I have no disposition to take long walks in such a state of the sky; nor have I any buoyancy of spirit. I am a very dull person just at this time.

September 25th.— .... One thing is certain. I cannot and will not spend the winter here. The time would be absolutely thrown away so far as regards any literary labour to be performed. . . . .

The intrusion of an outward necessity into labours of the imagination and intellect is, to me, very painful . . . .

I had rather a pleasant walk to a distant meadow a day or two ago, and we found white and purple grapes in great abundance, ripe, and gushing with rich, pure juice when the hand pressed the clusters. Did you know what treasures of wild grapes there are in this land? If we dwell here, we will make our own wine. . . . .

September 27th.— . . . Now, as to the affair with ——, I fully confide in your opinion that he intends to make an unequal bargain with poor, simple, innocent me,—never having doubted this myself. But how is he to accomplish it? I am not, nor shall be, the least in his power, whereas he is, to a certain extent, in mine. He might announce his projected Library, with me for the editor, in all the newspapers in the universe; but still I could not be bound to become the editor, unless by my own act; nor should I have the slightest scruple in refusing to be so, at the last moment, if he persisted in treating me with injustice. Then, as for his printing *Grandfather's Chair*, I have the copyright in my own hands, and could and would prevent the sale, or make him account to me for the profits, in case of need. Meantime he is making arrangements for publishing the Library, contracting with other booksellers, and with printers and engravers, and, with every step, making it more difficult for himself to draw back. I, on the other hand, do nothing which I should not do if the affair with —— were at an end : for, if I write a book, it will be just as available for some other publisher as for him. Instead of getting me into his power by this delay, he has trusted to my ignorance and simplicity, and has put *himself* in *my* power.

He is not insensible of this. At our last interview, he himself introduced the subject of the bargain, and appeared desirous to close it. But I was not prepared, —among other reasons, because I do not yet see what materials I shall have for the republications in the Library; the works that he has shown me being ill adapted for that purpose; and I wish first to see some French and German books which he has sent for to New York. And, before concluding the bargain, I have promised George Hillard to consult him, and let him do the business. Is not this consummate discretion? and am I not perfectly safe? .... I look at the matter with perfect composure, and see all round my own position, and know that it is impregnable.

* * * * *

I was elected to two high offices last night,—viz., to be a trustee of the Brook Farm estate, and Chairman of the Committee of Finance! ... From the nature of my office, I shall have the chief direction of all the money affairs of the community, the making of bargains, the supervision of receipts and expenditures, &c. &c. &c. ...

My accession to these august offices does not at all decide the question of my remaining here permanently. I told Mr. Ripley that I could not spend the winter at the farm, and that it was quite uncertain whether I returned in the spring. ...

Take no part, I beseech you, in these magnetic miracles. I am unwilling that a power should be exercised on you of which we know neither the origin nor consequence, and the phenomena of which seem rather calculated to bewilder us than to teach us any truths about the present or future state of being. ... Supposing that the power arises from the transfusion of one spirit into another, it seems to me that the sacredness of an individual is violated by it; there would be an intruder into the holy of holies. . . . I have no faith whatever that people are raised to the seventh heaven, or to any heaven at all, or that they gain any insight into the mysteries of life beyond death by means of this strange science. Without distrusting that the phenomena have really occurred, I think that they are to be accounted for as the result of a material and physical, not of a spiritual, influence. Opium has produced many a brighter vision of heaven, I fancy, and just as susceptible of proof as these. They are dreams. . . . And what delusion can be more lamentable and mischievous than to mistake the physical and material for the spiritual? what so miserable as to lose the soul's true, though hidden, knowledge and consciousness of heaven in the mist of an earth-born vision? If we would know what heaven is before we come thither, let us retire into the depths of our own spirits, and we shall find it there among holy thoughts and feelings; but let us not degrade high heaven and its inhabitants into any such symbols and forms as Miss L—— describes; do not let an earthly effluence from Mrs. P——'s corporeal system bewilder and perhaps contaminate something spiritual and sacred. I should as soon think of seeking revelations of the future state in the rottenness of the grave,—where so many do seek it. . . .

The view which I take of this matter is caused by no want of faith in mysteries; but from a deep reverence of the soul, and of the mysteries which it knows within itself, but never transmits to the earthly eye and ear. Keep the imagination sane,— that is one of the truest conditions of communion with heaven.

Brook Farm, September 26th.—A walk this morning along the Needham road. A clear, breezy morning, after nearly a week of cloudy and showery weather. The grass is much more fresh and vivid than it was last month, and trees still retain much of their verdure, though here and there is a shrub or a bough arrayed in scarlet and gold. Along the road, in the midst of a beaten track, I saw mushrooms or toadstools, which had sprung up probably during the night.

The houses in this vicinity are, many of them, quite antique, with long sloping roofs, commencing at a few feet from the ground, and ending in a lofty peak. Some of them have huge old elms overshadowing the yard. One may see the family sleigh near the door, it having stood there all through the summer sunshine, and perhaps with weeds sprouting through the crevices of its bottom, the growth of the months since snow departed. Old barns, patched and supported by timbers leaning against the sides, and stained with the excrement of past ages.

In the forenoon I walked along the edge of the meadow towards Cow Island. Large trees, almost a wood, principally of pine with the green pasture-glades intermixed, and cattle feeding. They cease grazing when an intruder appears, and look at him with long and wary observation, then bend their heads to the pasture again. Where the firm ground of the pasture ceases, the meadow begins,—loose, spongy, yielding to the tread, sometimes permitting the foot to sink into black mud, or perhaps over ankles in water. Cattle-paths, somewhat firmer than the general surface, traverse the dense shrubbery which has overgrown the meadow. This shrubbery consists of small birch, elders, maples, and other trees, with here and there white pines of larger growth. The whole is tangled and wild and thick-set, so that it is necessary to part the nestling stems and branches, and go crashing through. There are creeping plants of various sorts which clamber up the trees ; and some of them have changed colour in the slight frosts which already have befallen these low grounds, so that one sees a spiral wreath of scarlet leaves twining up to the top of a green tree, intermingling its bright hues with their verdure, as if all were of one piece. Sometimes, instead of scarlet, the spiral wreath is of a golden yellow.

Within the verge of the meadow, mostly near the firm shore of pasture ground, I found several grapevines, hung with an abundance of large purple grapes. The vines had caught hold of maples and alders, and climbed to the summit, curling round about and interwreathing their twisted folds in so intimate a manner that it was not easy to tell the parasite from the supporting tree or shrub. Sometimes the same vine had enveloped several shrubs, and caused a strange, tangled confusion, converting all these poor plants to the purpose of its own support, and hindering their growing to their own benefit and convenience. The broad vine-leaves, some of them yellow or yellowish-tinged, were seen apparently growing on the same stems with the silver-maple leaves, and those of the other shrubs, thus married against their will by the conjugal twine ; and the purple clusters of grapes hung down from above and in the midst, so that one might "gather grapes," if not "of thorns," yet of as alien bushes.

One vine had ascended almost to the tip of a large white pine, spreading its leaves and hanging its purple clusters among all its boughs,—still climbing and clambering, as if it would not be content till it had crowned the very summit with a wreath of its own foliage and bunches of grapes. I mounted high into the tree, and ate the fruit there, while the vine wreathed still higher into the depths above my head. The grapes were sour, being not yet fully ripe. Some of them, however, were sweet and pleasant.

September 27th.—A ride to Brighton yesterday morning, it being the day of the weekly cattle-fair. William Allen and myself went in a waggon, carrying a calf to be sold at the fair. The calf had not had his breakfast, as his mother had preceded him to Brighton, and he kept expressing his hunger and discomfort by loud, sonorous baas, especially when we passed any cattle in the fields or in the road. The cows, grazing within hearing, expressed great interest, and some of them came galloping to the roadside to behold the calf. Little children, also, on their way to school, stopped to laugh and point at poor little Bossie. He was a prettily behaved urchin, and kept thrusting his hairy muzzle between William and myself, apparently wishing to be stroked and patted. It was an ugly thought that his confidence in human nature, and nature in general, was to be so ill rewarded as by cutting his throat, and selling him in quarters. This, I suppose, has been his fate before now.

It was a beautiful morning, clear as crystal, with an invigorating, but not disagreeable coolness. The general aspect of the country was as green as summer, —greener indeed than mid or latter summer,—and there were occasional interminglings of the brilliant hues of autumn, which made the scenery more beautiful, both visibly and in sentiment. We saw no absolutely mean nor poor-looking abodes along the road. There were warm and comfortable farmhouses, ancient, with the porch, the sloping roof, the antique peak, the clustered chimney, of old times ; and modern cottages, smart and tasteful ; and villas, with terraces before them, and dense shade, and wooden urns on pillars, and other such tokens of gentility. Pleasant groves of oak and walnut, also, there were, sometimes stretching along valleys, sometimes ascending a hill and clothing it all round, so as to make it a great clump of verdure. Frequently we passed people with cows, oxen, sheep, or pigs for Brighton Fair.

On arriving at Brighton, we found the village thronged with people, horses, and vehicles. Probably there is no place in New England where the character of an agricultural population may be so well studied. Almost all the farmers within a reasonable distance make it a point, I suppose, to attend Brighton Fair pretty frequently, if not on business, yet as amateurs. Then there are all the cattle-people and butchers who supply the Boston market, and dealers from far and near; and every man who has a cow or a yoke of oxen, whether to sell or buy, goes to Brighton on Monday. There were a thousand or two of cattle in the extensive pens belonging to the tavern-keeper, besides many that were standing about. One could hardly stir a step without running upon the horns of one dilemma or another, in the shape of ox, cow, bull, or ram. The yeomen appeared to be more in their element than I have ever seen them anywhere else, except, indeed, at labour,—more so than at musterings and such gatherings of amusement. And yet this was a sort of festal day, as well as a day of business. Most of the people were of a bulky make, with much bone and muscle, and some good store of fat, as if they had lived on flesh-diet; with mottled faces, too, hard and red, like those of persons who adhered to the old fashion of spirit-drinking. Great, round-paunched country squires were there too, sitting under the porch of the tavern, or waddling about, whip in hand, discussing the points of the cattle. There were also gentlemen-farmers, neatly, trimly, and fashionably dressed, in handsome surtouts and trousers, strapped under their boots. Yeomen, too, in their black or blue Sunday suits, cut by country tailors, and awkwardly worn. Others (like myself) had on the blue stuff frocks which they wear in the fields, the most comfortable garments that ever were invented. Country loafers were among the throng,— men who looked wistfully at the liquors in the bar, and waited for some friend to invite them to drink,— poor, shabby, out-at-elbowed devils. Also, dandies from the city, corseted and buckramed, who had come to see the humours of Brighton Fair. All these, and other varieties of mankind, either thronged the spacious bar-room of the hotel, drinking, smoking, talking, bargaining, or walked about among the cattle-pens, looking with knowing eyes at the horned people. The owners of the cattle stood near at hand, waiting for offers. There was something indescribable in their aspect, that showed them to be the owners, though they mixed among the crowd. The cattle, brought from a hundred separate farms, or rather from a thousand, seemed to agree very well together, not quarrelling in the least. They almost all had a history, no doubt, if they could but have told it. The cows had each given her milk to support families, —had roamed the pastures, and come home to the barn-yard, had been looked upon as a sort of member of the domestic circle, and was known by a name, as Brindle or Cherry. The oxen, with their necks bent by the heavy yoke, had toiled in the plough-field and in haying-time for many years, and knew their master's stall as well as the master himself knew his own table. Even the young steers and the little calves had something of domestic sacredness about them; for children had watched their growth, and petted them, and played with them. And here they all were, old and young, gathered from their thousand homes to Brighton Fair; whence the great chance was that they would go to the slaughter-house, and thence be transmitted, in sirloins, joints, and such pieces, to the tables of the Boston folk.

William Allen had come to buy four little pigs to take the places of four who have now grown large at our farm, and are to be fatted and killed within a few weeks. There were several hundreds, in pens appropriated to their use, grunting discordantly, and apparently in no very good humour with their companions or the world at large. Most or many of these pigs had been imported from the State of New York. The drovers set out with a large number, and peddle them along the road till they arrive at Brighton with the remainder. William selected four, and bought them at five cents. per pound. These poor little porkers were forthwith seized by the tails, their legs tied, and they thrown into our waggon, where they kept up a continual grunt and squeal till we got home. Two of them were yellowish, or light gold-colour, the other two were black and white, speckled; and all four of very piggish aspect and deportment. One of them snapped at William's finger most spitefully, and bit it to the bone.

All the scene of the fair was very characteristic and peculiar,—cheerful and lively, too, in the bright, warm sun. I must see it again; for it ought to be studied.

September 28*th*.—A picnic party in the woods, yesterday, in honour of little Frank Dana's birthday, he being six years old. I strolled out, after dinner, with Mr. Bradford, and in a lonesome glade we met the apparition of an Indian chief, dressed in appropriate costume of blanket, feathers, and paint, and armed with a musket. Almost at the same time, a young gipsy fortune-teller came from among the trees, and proposed to tell my fortune. While she was doing this, the goddess Diana let fly an arrow, and hit me smartly in the hand. The fortune-teller and goddess were in fine contrast: Diana being a blonde, fair, quiet, with a moderate composure; and the gipsy (O. G.) a bright, vivacious, dark-haired, rich-complexioned damsel,—both of them very pretty, at least pretty enough to make fifteen years enchanting. Accompanied by these denizens of the wildwood, we went onward, and came to a company of fantastic figures, arranged in a ring for a dance or a game. There was a Swiss girl, an Indian squaw, a negro of the Jim Crow order, one or two foresters, and several people in Christian attire, besides children of all ages. Then followed childish games, in which the grown people took part with mirth enough, while I, whose nature it is to be a mere spectator both of sport and serious business, lay under the trees and looked on. Meanwhile, Mr. Emerson and Miss Fuller, who arrived an hour or two before, came forth into the little glade where we were assembled. Here followed much talk. The ceremonies of the day concluded with a cold collation of cakes and fruit. All was pleasant enough,—an excellent piece of work, —" would 'twere done!" It has left a fantastic impression on my memory, this intermingling of wild and fabulous characters with real and homely ones, in the secluded nook of the woods. I remember them, with the sunlight breaking through overshadowing branches, and they appearing and disappearing confusedly,—perhaps starting out of the earth; as if the every-day laws of Nature were suspended for this particular occasion. There were the children, too, laughing and sporting about, as if they were at home among such strange shapes,—and anon bursting into loud uproar of lamentation, when the rude gambols of the merry archers chanced to overturn them. And apart, with a shrewd, Yankee observation of the scene, stands our friend Orange, a thick-set, sturdy figure, enjoying the fun well enough, yet rather laughing with a perception of its nonsensicalness than at all entering into the spirit of the thing.

This morning I have been helping to gather

apples. The principal farm labours at this time are ploughing for winter rye, and breaking up the greensward for next year's crop of potatoes, gathering squashes, and not much else, except such year-round employments as milking. The crop of rye, to be sure, is in process of being thrashed, at odd intervals.

I ought to have mentioned among the diverse and incongruous growths of the picnic party our two Spanish boys from Manilla;—Lucas, with his heavy features and almost mulatto complexion; and José, slighter, with rather a feminine face,—not a gay, girlish one, but grave, reserved, eyeing you sometimes with an earnest but secret expression, and causing you to question what sort of person he is.

Friday, October 1st.—I have been looking at our four swine,—not of the last lot, but those in process of fattening. They lie among the clean rye straw in the sty, nestling close together; for they seem to be beasts sensitive to the cold, and this is a clear, bright, crystal morning, with a cool north-west wind. So there lie these four black swine, as deep among the straw as they can burrow, the very symbols of slothful ease and sensuous comfort. They seem to be actually oppressed and overburdened with comfort. They are quick to notice any one's approach, and utter a low grunt thereupon,—not drawing a breath for that particular purpose, but grunting with their ordinary breath,—at the same time turning an observant, though dull and sluggish, eye upon the visitor. They seem to be involved and buried in their own corporeal substance, and to look dimly forth at the outer world. They breathe not easily, and yet not with difficulty nor discomfort; for the very unreadiness and oppression with which their breath comes appears to make them sensible of the deep sensual satisfaction which they feel. Swill, the remnant of their last meal, remains in the trough, denoting that their food is more abundant than even a hog can demand. Anon they fall asleep, drawing short and heavy breaths, which heave their huge sides up and down; but at the slightest noise they sluggishly unclose their eyes, and give another gentle grunt. They also grunt among themselves, without any external cause; but merely to express their swinish sympathy. I suppose it is the knowledge that these four grunters are doomed to die within two or three weeks that gives them a sort of awfulness in my conception. It makes me contrast their present gross substance of fleshly life with the nothingness speedily to come. Meantime the four newly-bought pigs are running about the cow-yard, lean, active, shrewd, investigating everything, as their nature is. When I throw an apple among them, they scramble with one another for the prize, and the successful one scampers away to eat it at leisure. They thrust their snouts into the mud, and pick a grain of corn out of the rubbish. Nothing within their sphere do they leave unexamined, grunting all the time with infinite variety of expression. Their language is the most copious of that of any quadruped, and, indeed, there is something deeply and indefinably interesting in the swinish race. They appear the more a mystery the longer one gazes at them. It seems as if there were an important meaning to them, if one could but find it out. One interesting trait in them is their perfect independence of character. They care not for man, and will not adapt themselves to his notions, as other beasts do; but are true to themselves, and act out their hoggish nature.

October 7th.—Since Saturday last (it being now Thursday), I have been in Boston and Salem, and there has been a violent storm and rain during the whole time. This morning shone as bright as if it meant to make up for all the dismalness of the past days. Our brook, which in the summer was no longer a running stream, but stood in pools along its pebbly course, is now full from one grassy verge to the other, and hurries along with a murmuring rush. It will continue to swell, I suppose, and in the winter and spring it will flood all the broad meadows through which it flows.

I have taken a long walk this forenoon along the Needham road, and across the bridge, thence pursuing a cross-road through the woods, parallel with the river, which I crossed again at Dedham. Most of the road lay through a growth of young oaks principally. They still retain their verdure, though, looking closely in among them, one perceives the broken sunshine falling on a few sere or bright-hued tufts of shrubbery. In low, marshy spots, on the verge of the meadows or along the river-side, there is a much more marked autumnal change. Whole ranges of bushes are there painted with many variegated hues, not of the brightest tint, but of a sober cheerfulness. I suppose this is owing more to the late rains than to the frost; for a heavy rain changes the foliage somewhat at this season. The first marked frost was seen last Saturday morning. Soon after sunrise it lay, white as snow, over all the grass, and on the tops of the fences, and in the yard, on the heap of firewood. On Sunday, I think, there was a fall of snow, which, however, did not lie on the ground a moment.

There is no season when such pleasant and sunny spots may be lighted on, and produce so pleasant an effect on the feelings, as now in October. The sunshine is peculiarly genial, and in sheltered places, as on the side of a bank, or of a barn or house, one becomes acquainted and friendly with the sunshine. It seems to be of a kindly and homely nature. And the green grass, strewn with a few withered leaves, looks the more green and beautiful for them. In summer or spring, Nature is farther from one's sympathies.

October 8th.—Another gloomy day, lowering with portents of rain close at hand. I have walked up into the pastures this morning, and looked about me a little. The woods present a very diversified appearance just now, with perhaps more varieties of tint than they are destined to wear at a somewhat later period. There are some strong yellow hues, and some deep red ; there are innumerable shades of green, some few having the depth of summer ; others, partially changed towards yellow, look freshly verdant with the delicate tinge of early summer or of May. Then there is the solemn and dark green of the pines. The effect is, that every tree in the wood and every bush among the shrubbery has a separate existence, since, confusedly intermingled, each wears its peculiar colour, instead of being lost in the universal emerald of summer. And yet there is a oneness of effect likewise, when we choose to look at a whole sweep of woodland instead of analysing its component trees. Scattered over the pasture, which the late rains have kept tolerably green, there are spots or islands of dusky red,—a deep, substantial hue, very well fit to be close to the ground,—while the yellow, and light, fantastic shades of green soar upward to the sky. These red spots are the blueberry and whortleberry bushes. The sweet-fern is changed mostly to russet, but still retains its wild and delightful fragrance when pressed in the hand. Wild China-asters are scattered about, but beginning to wither. A little while ago, mushrooms or toadstools were very numerous along the wood-paths and by the roadsides, especially after rain. Some were of spotless white, some yellow, and some scarlet. They are always mysteries and objects of interest to me, springing as they do so suddenly from no root or seed, and growing one wonders why. I think, too, that some varieties are pretty objects, little fairy tables, centre-tables, standing on one leg. But their growth appears to be checked now, and they are of a brown tint and decayed.

The farm business to-day is to dig potatoes. I worked a little at it. The process is to grasp all the stems of a hill and pull them up. A great many of the potatoes are thus pulled, clinging to the stems and to one another in curious shapes,—long red things, and little round ones, embedded in the earth which clings to the roots. These being plucked off, the rest of the potatoes are dug out of the hill with a hoe, the tops being flung into a heap for the cowyard. On my way home I paused to inspect the squash-field. Some of the squashes lay in heaps as they were gathered, presenting much variety of shape and hue,—as golden yellow, like great lumps of gold, dark green, striped and variegated; and some were round, and some lay curling their long necks, nestling, as it were, and seeming as if they had life.

In my walk yesterday forenoon I passed an old house which seemed to be quite deserted. It was a two-story, wooden house, dark and weather-beaten. The front windows, some of them, were shattered and open, and others were boarded up. Trees and shrubbery were growing neglected, so as quite to block up the lower part. There was an aged barn near at hand, so ruinous that it had been necessary to prop it up. There were two old carts, both of which had lost a wheel. Everything was in keeping. At first I supposed that there would be no inhabitants in such a dilapidated place ; but, passing on, I looked back, and saw a decrepit and infirm old man at the angle of the house, its fit occupant. The grass, however, was very green and beautiful around this dwelling, and, the sunshine falling brightly on it, the whole effect was cheerful and pleasant. It seemed as if the world was so glad that this desolate old place, where there was never to be any more hope and happiness, could not at all lessen the general effect of joy.

I found a small turtle by the roadside, where he had crept to warm himself in the genial sunshine. He had a sable back, and underneath his shell was yellow, and at the edges bright scarlet. His head, tail, and claws were striped yellow, black, and red. He withdrew himself as far as he possibly could into his shell, and absolutely refused to peep out, even when I put him into the water. Finally, I threw him into a deep pool and left him. These mailed gentlemen, from the size of a foot or more down to an inch, were very numerous in the spring; and now the smaller kind appear again.

Saturday, October 9th.—Still dismal weather. Our household, being composed in great measure of children and young people, is generally a cheerful one enough, even in gloomy weather. For a week past we have been especially gladdened with a little seamstress from Boston, about seventeen years old; but of such a *petite* figure that, at first view, one would take her to be hardly in her teens. She is very vivacious and smart, laughing and singing and talking all the time,—talking sensibly; but still, taking the view of matters that a city girl naturally would. If she were larger than she is, and of less pleasing aspect, I think she might be intolerable; but being so small, and with a fair skin, and as healthy as a wild-flower, she is really very agreeable; and to look at her face is like being shone upon by a ray of the sun. She never walks, but bounds and dances along, and this motion, in her diminutive person, does not give the idea of violence. It is like a bird, hopping from twig to twig, and chirping merrily all the time. Sometimes she is rather vulgar, but even that works well enough into her character, and accords with it. On continued observation, one discovers that she is not a little girl, but really a little woman, with all the prerogatives and liabilities of a woman. This gives a new aspect to her, while the girlish impression still remains, and is strangely combined with the sense that this frolicksome maiden has the material for the sober bearing of a wife. She romps with the boys, runs races with them in the yard, and up and down the stairs, and is heard scolding laughingly at their rough play. She asks William Allen to place her "on top of that horse," whereupon he puts his large brown hands about her waist, and, swinging her to and fro, lifts her on horseback. William threatens to rivet two horse-shoes round her neck, for having clambered, with the other girls and boys, upon a load of hay, whereby the said load lost its balance and slid off the cart. She strings the seed-berries of roses together, making a scarlet necklace of them, which she fastens about her throat. She gathers flowers of everlasting to wear in her bonnet, arranging them with the skill of a dressmaker. In the evening, she sits singing by the hour, with the musical part of the establishment, often breaking into laughter, whereto she is incited by the tricks of the boys. The last thing one hears of her, she is tripping upstairs to bed, talking lightsomely or warbling; and one meets her in the morning, the very image of bright morn itself, smiling briskly at you, so that one takes her for a promise of cheerfulness through the day. Be it said, with all the rest, that there is a perfect maiden modesty in her deportment. She has just gone away, and the last I saw of her was her vivacious face peeping through the curtain of the cariole, and nodding a gay farewell to the family, who were shouting their adieus at the door. With her other merits, she is an excellent daughter, and supports her mother by the labour of her hands. It would be difficult to conceive beforehand how much can be added to the enjoyment of a household by mere sunniness of temper and liveliness of disposition; for her intellect is very ordinary, and she never says anything worth hearing, or even laughing at, in itself. But she herself is an expression well worth studying.

Brook Farm, October 9th.—A walk this afternoon

to Cow Island. The clouds had broken away towards noon, and let forth a few sunbeams, and more and more blue sky ventured to appear, till at last it was really warm and sunny,—indeed, rather too warm in the sheltered hollows, though it is delightful to be too warm now, after so much stormy chillness. Oh, the beauty of grassy slopes, and the hollow ways of paths winding between hills, and the intervals between the road and wood-lots, where Summer lingers and sits down, strewing dandelions of gold, and blue asters, as her parting gifts and memorials! I went to a grape-vine, which I have already visited several times, and found some clusters of grapes still remaining, and now perfectly ripe. Coming within view of the river, I saw several wild ducks under the shadow of the opposite shore, which was high, and covered with a grove of pines. I should not have discovered the ducks had they not risen and skimmed the surface of the glassy stream, breaking its dark water with a bright streak, and, sweeping round, gradually rose high enough to fly away. I likewise started a partridge just within the verge of the woods, and in another place a large squirrel ran across the wood-path from one shelter of trees to the other. Small birds, in flocks, were flitting about the fields, seeking and finding I know not what sort of food. There were little fish, also, darting in shoals through the pools and depths of the brooks, which are now replenished to their brims, and rush towards the river with a swift, amber-coloured current.

Cow Island is not an island,—at least, at this season,—though, I believe, in the time of freshets, the marshy Charles floods the meadows all round about it, and extends across its communication with the main-land. The path to it is a very secluded one, threading a wood of pines, and just wide enough to admit the loads of meadow hay which are drawn from the splashy shore of the river. The Island has a growth of stately pines, with tall and ponderous stems, standing at distance enough to admit the eye to travel far among them; and, as there is no underbrush, the effect is somewhat like looking among the pillars of a church.

I returned home by the high-road. On my right, separated from the road by a level field, perhaps fifty yards across, was a range of young forest-trees, dressed in their garb of autumnal glory. The sun shone directly upon them; and sunlight is like the breath of life to the pomp of autumn. In its absence, one doubts whether there be any truth in what poets have told about the splendour of an American autumn; but when this charm is added, one feels that the effect is beyond description. As I beheld it to-day, there was nothing dazzling; it was gentle and mild, though brilliant and diversified, and had a most quiet and pensive influence. And yet there were some trees that seemed really made of sunshine, and others were of a sunny red, and the whole picture was painted with but little relief of darksome hues,—only a few evergreens. But there was nothing inharmonious; and, on closer examination, it appeared that all the tints had a relationship among themselves. And this, I suppose, is the reason that, while Nature seems to scatter them so carelessly, they still never shock the beholder by their contrasts, nor disturb, but only soothe. The brilliant scarlet and the brilliant yellow are different hues of the maple-leaves, and the first changes into the last. I saw one maple-tree, its centre yellow as gold, set in a framework of red. The native poplars have different shades of green, verging towards yellow, and are very cheerful in the sunshine. Most of the oak-leaves have still the deep verdure of summer; but where a change has taken place, it is into a russet-red, warm, but sober. These colours, infinitely varied by the progress which different trees have made in their decay, constitute almost the whole glory of autumnal woods ; but it is impossible to conceive how much is done with such scanty materials. In my whole walk I saw only one man, and he was at a distance, in the obscurity of the trees. He had a horse and a waggon, and was getting a load of dry brushwood.

Sunday, October 10*th.*—I visited my grape-vine this afternoon, and ate the last of its clusters. This vine climbs around a young maple-tree, which has now assumed the yellow leaf. The leaves of the vine are more decayed than those of the maple. Thence to Cow Island, a solemn and thoughtful walk. Returned by another path of the width of a waggon, passing through a grove of hard wood, the lightsome hues of which make the walk more cheerful than among the pines. The roots of oaks emerged from the soil, and contorted themselves across the path. The sunlight, also, broke across in spots, and otherwheres the shadow was deep ; but still there was intermingling enough of bright hues to keep off the gloom from the whole path.

Brooks and pools have a peculiar aspect at this season. One knows that the water must be cold, and one shivers a little at the sight of it; and yet the grass about the pool may be of the deepest green, and the sun may be shining into it. The withered leaves which overhanging trees shed upon its surface contribute much to the effect.

Insects have mostly vanished in the fields and woods. I hear locusts yet, singing in the sunny hours, and crickets have not yet finished their song. Once in a while I see a caterpillar,—this afternoon, for instance, a red, hairy one, with black head and tail. They do not appear to be active, and it makes one rather melancholy to look at them.

Tuesday, October 12*th.*—The cawing of the crow resounds among the woods. A sentinel is aware of your approach a great way off, and gives the alarm to his comrades loudly and eagerly,—Caw, caw, caw! Immediately the whole conclave replies, and you behold them rising above the trees, flapping darkly, and winging their way to deeper solitudes. Sometimes, however, they remain till you come near enough to discern their sable gravity of aspect, each occupying a separate bough, or perhaps the blasted tip-top of a pine. As you approach, one after another, with loud cawing, flaps his wings and throws himself upon the air.

There is hardly a more striking feature in the landscape now-a-days than the red patches of blueberry and whortleberry bushes, as seen on a sloping hillside, like islands among the grass, with trees growing in them; or crowning the summit of a bare brown hill with their somewhat russet liveliness; or circling round the base of an earth-embedded rock. At a distance, this hue, clothing spots and patches of the earth, looks more like a picture than anything else,—yet such a picture as I never saw painted.

The oaks are now beginning to look sere, and their leaves have withered borders. It is pleasant to notice the wide circle of greener grass beneath the circumference of an overshadowing oak. Passing an orchard, one hears an uneasy rustling in the trees, and not as if they were struggling with the wind. Scattered about are barrels to contain the gathered apples; and perhaps a great heap of golden or scarlet apples is collected in one place.

Wednesday, October 13th.—A good view, from an upland swell of our pasture, across the valley of the river Charles. There is the meadow, as level as a floor, and carpeted with green, perhaps two miles from the rising ground on this side of the river to that on the opposite side. The stream winds through the midst of the flat space, without any banks at all; for it fills its bed almost to the brim, and bathes the meadow grass on either side. A tuft of shrubbery, at broken intervals, is scattered along its border; and thus it meanders sluggishly along, without other life than what it gains from gleaming in the sun. Now, into the broad, smooth meadow, as into a lake, capes and headlands put themselves forth, and shores of firm woodland border it, covered with variegated foliage, making the contrast so much the stronger of their height and rough outline with the even spread of the plain. And beyond, and far away, rises a long, gradual swell of country, covered with an apparently dense growth of foliage for miles, till the horizon terminates it; and here and there is a house, or perhaps two, among the contiguity of trees. Everywhere the trees wear their autumnal dress, so that the whole landscape is red, russet, orange, and yellow, blending in the distance into a rich tint of brown-orange, or nearly that,—except the green expanse so definitely hemmed in by the higher ground.

I took a long walk this morning, going first nearly to Newton, thence nearly to Brighton, thence to Jamaica Plain, and thence home. It was a fine morning, with a north-west wind; cool when facing the wind, but warm and most genially pleasant in sheltered spots; and warm enough everywhere while I was in motion. I traversed most of the by-ways which offered themselves to me; and, passing through one in which there was a double line of grass between the wheel-tracks and that of the horses' feet, I came to where had once stood a farm-house, which appeared to have been recently torn down. Most of the old timber and boards had been carted away; a pile of it, however, remained. The cellar of the house was uncovered, and beside it stood the base and middle height of the chimney. The oven, in which household bread had been baked for daily food, and puddings and cake and jolly pumpkin-pies for festivals, opened its mouth, being deprived of its iron door. The fire-place was close at hand. All round the site of the house was a pleasant, sunny, green space, with old fruit-trees in pretty fair condition, though aged. There was a barn, also aged, but in decent repair; and a ruinous shed, on the corner of which was nailed a boy's windmill, where it had probably been turning and clattering for years together, till now it was black with time and weather-stain. It was broken, but still it went round whenever the wind stirred. The spot was entirely secluded, there being no other house within a mile or two.

No language can give an idea of the beauty and glory of the trees just at this moment. It would be easy, by a process of word-daubing, to set down a confused group of gorgeous colours, like a bunch of tangled skeins of bright silk; but there is nothing of the reality in the glare which would thus be produced. And yet the splendour both of individual clusters and of whole scenes is unsurpassable. The oaks are now far advanced in their change of hue; and, in certain positions relatively to the sun, they light up and gleam with a most magnificent deep gold, varying according as portions of the foliage are in shadow or sunlight. On the sides which receive the direct rays, the effect is altogether rich; and in other points of view it is equally beautiful, if less brilliant. This colour of the oak is more superb than the lighter yellow of the maples and walnuts. The whole landscape is now covered with this indescribable pomp; it is discerned on the uplands afar off; and Blue Hill, in Milton, at the distance of several miles, actually glistens with rich, dark light,—no, not glistens, nor gleams,—but perhaps to say glows subduedly will be a truer expression for it.

Met few people this morning; a grown girl, in company with a little boy, gathering barberries in a secluded lane; a portly, autumnal gentleman, wrapped in a great-coat, who asked the way to Mr. Joseph Goddard's; and a fish-cart from the city, the driver of which sounded his horn along the lonesome way.

Monday, October 18*th.*—There has been a succession of days which were cold and bright in the forenoon, and gray, sullen, and chill towards night. The woods have now taken a soberer tint than they wore at my last date. Many of the shrubs which looked brightest a little while ago are now wholly bare of leaves. The oaks have generally a russet-brown shade, although some of them are still green, as are likewise other scattered trees in the forests. The bright yellow and the rich scarlet are no more to be seen. Scarcely any of them will now bear a close examination; for this shows them to be rugged, wilted, and of faded, frost-bitten hue; but at a distance, and in the mass, and enlivened by the sun, they have still somewhat of the varied splendour which distinguished them a week ago. It is wonderful what a difference the sunshine makes; it is like varnish, bringing out the hidden veins in a piece of rich wood. In the cold, grey atmosphere, such as that of most of our afternoons now, the landscape lies dark,—brown, and in a much deeper shadow than if it were clothed in green. But, perchance, a gleam of sun falls on a certain spot of distant shrubbery or woodland, and we see it brighten with many hues, standing forth prominently from the dimness around it. The sunlight gradually spreads, and the whole sombre scene is changed to a motley picture,—the sun bringing out many shades of colour, and converting its gloom to an almost laughing cheerfulness. At such times I almost doubt whether the foliage has lost any of its brilliancy. But the clouds intercept the sun again, and lo! old Autumn appears, clad in his cloak of russet-brown.

Beautiful now, while the general landscape lies in shadow, looks the summit of a distant hill (say a mile off), with the sunshine brightening the trees that cover it. It is noticeable that the outlines of hills, and the whole bulk of them at the distance of several miles, become stronger, denser, and more substantial in this autumn atmosphere and in these autumnal tints than in summer. Then they looked blue, misty, and dim. Now they show their great humpbacks more plainly, as if they had drawn nearer to us.

A waste of shrubbery and small trees, such as overruns the borders of the meadows for miles together, looks much more rugged, wild, and savage in its present brown colour than when clad in green.

I passed through a very pleasant wood-path yesterday, quite shut in and sheltered by trees that had not thrown off their yellow robes. The sun shone strongly in among them, and quite kindled them; so that the path was brighter for their shade than if it had been quite exposed to the sun.

In the village graveyard, which lies contiguous to the street, I saw a man digging a grave, and one inhabitant after another turned aside from his way to look into the grave and talk with the digger. I heard him laugh, with the traditionary mirthfulness of men of that occupation.

In the hollow of the woods, yesterday afternoon, I lay a long while watching a squirrel, who was capering about among the trees over my head (oaks and white-pines, so close together that their branches intermingled). The squirrel seemed not to approve of my presence, for he frequently uttered a sharp, quick, angry noise, like that of a scissors-grinder's wheel.

Sometimes I could see him sitting on an impending bough, with his tail over his back, looking down pryingly upon me. It seems to be a natural posture with him to sit on his hind-legs, holding up his forepaws. Anon, with a peculiarly quick start, he would scramble along the branch, and be lost to sight in another part of the tree, whence his shrill chatter would again be heard. Then I would see him rapidly descending the trunk, and running along the ground; and a moment afterwards, casting my eye upward, I beheld him flitting like a bird among the high limbs at the summit, directly above me. Afterwards, he apparently became accustomed to my society, and set about some business of his own. He came down to the ground, took up a piece of a decayed bough (a heavy burden for such a small personage), and, with this in his mouth, again climbed up and passed from the branches of one tree to those of another, and thus onward and onward till he went out of sight. Shortly afterwards he returned for another burden, and this he repeated several times. I suppose he was building a nest,—at least, I know not what else could have been his object. Never was there such an active, cheerful, choleric, continually-in-motion fellow as this little red squirrel, talking to himself, chattering at me, and as sociable in his own person as if he had half a dozen companions, instead of being alone in the lonesome wood. Indeed, he flitted about so quickly, and showed himself in different places so suddenly, that I was in some doubt whether there were not two or three of them.

I must mention again the very beautiful effect produced by the masses of berry-bushes, lying like scarlet islands in the midst of withered pasture-ground, or crowning the tops of barren hills. Their hue, at a distance, is lustrous scarlet, although it does not look nearly as bright and gorgeous when examined close at hand. But at a proper distance it is a beautiful fringe on Autumn's petticoat.

Friday, October 22nd.—A continued succession of unpleasant, Novembery days, and autumn has made rapid progress in the work of decay. It is now somewhat of a rare good fortune to find a verdant, grassy spot, on some slope, or in a dell; and even such seldom-seen oases are bestrewn with dried brown leaves,—which, however, methinks, make the short, fresh grass look greener around them. Dry leaves are now plentiful everywhere, save where there are none but pine-trees. They rustle beneath the tread, and there is nothing more autumnal than that sound.

Nevertheless, in a walk this afternoon I have seen two oaks which retained almost the greenness of summer. They grew close to the huge Pulpit Rock, so that portions of their trunks appeared to grasp the rough surface; and they were rooted beneath it, and, ascending high into the air, overshadowed the gray crag with verdure. Other oaks, here and there, have a few green leaves or boughs among their rustling and rugged shade.

Yet, dreary as the woods are in a bleak, sullen day, there is a very peculiar sense of warmth and a sort of richness of effect in the slope of a bank and in sheltered spots, where bright sunshine falls, and the brown oaken foliage is gladdened by it. There is then a feeling of comfort, and consequently of heart-warmth, which cannot be experienced in summer.

I walked this afternoon along a pleasant wood-path, gently winding, so that but little of it could be seen at a time, and going up and down small mounds, now plunging into a denser shadow, and now emerging from it. Part of the way it was strewn with the dusky, yellow leaves of white-pines,—the cast-off garments of last year; part of the way with green grass, close-cropped, and very fresh for the season. Sometimes the trees met across it; sometimes it was bordered on one side by an old rail-fence of moss-grown cedar, with bushes sprouting beneath it, and thrusting their branches through it; sometimes by a stone wall of unknown antiquity, older than the wood it closed in. A stone wall, when shrubbery has grown around it, and thrust its roots beneath it, becomes a very pleasant and meditative object. It does not belong too evidently to man, having been built so long ago. It seems a part of nature.

Yesterday I found two mushrooms in the woods, probably of the preceding night's growth. Also I saw a mosquito, frost-pinched, and so wretched that I felt avenged for all the injuries which his tribe inflicted upon me last summer, and so did not molest this lone survivor.

Walnuts in their green rinds are falling from the trees, and so are chestnut-burrs.

I found a maple-leaf to-day, yellow all over, except its extremest point, which was bright scarlet. It looked as if a drop of blood were hanging from it. The first change of the maple-leaf is to scarlet; the next to yellow. Then it withers, wilts, and drops off, as most of them have already done.

October 27th.—Fringed gentians,—I found the last,

probably, that will be seen this year, growing on the margin of the brook.

1842.—Some man of powerful character to command a person, morally subjected to him, to perform some act. The commanding person suddenly to die; and, for all the rest of his life, the subjected one continues to perform that act.

"Solomon dies during the building of the Temple, but his body remains leaning on a staff, and overlooking the workmen, as if it were alive."

A tri-weekly paper, to be called the Tertian Ague.

Subject for a picture,—Satan's reappearance in Pandemonium, shining out from a mist, with "shape star-bright."

Five points of Theology,—Five Points at New York.

It seems a greater pity that an accomplished worker with the hand should perish prematurely, than a person of great intellect; because intellectual arts may be cultivated in the next world, but not physical ones.

To trace out the influence of a frightful and disgraceful crime in debasing and destroying a character naturally high and noble, the guilty person being alone conscious of the crime.

A man, virtuous in his general conduct, but committing habitually some monstrous crime,—as murder,—and doing this without the sense of guilt, but with a peaceful conscience,—habit, probably, reconciling him to it; but something (for instance, discovery) occurs to make him sensible of his enormity. His horror then.

The strangeness, if they could be foreseen and forethought, of events which do not seem so strange after they have happened. As, for instance, to muse over a child's cradle, and foresee all the persons in different parts of the world with whom he would have relations.

A man to swallow a small snake,—and it to be a symbol of a cherished sin.

Questions as to unsettled points of history, and mysteries of nature, to be asked of a mesmerized person.

Gordier, a young man of the Island of Jersey, was paying his addresses to a young lady of Guernsey. He visited the latter island, intending to be married. He disappeared on his way from the beach to his mistress's residence, and was afterwards found dead in a cavity of the rocks. After a time, Galliard, a merchant of Guernsey, paid his addresses to the young lady; but she always felt a strong, unaccountable antipathy to him. He presented her with a beautiful trinket. The mother of Gordier, chancing to see this trinket, recognized it as having been bought by her dead son as a present for his mistress. She expired on learning this; and Galliard, being suspected of the murder, committed suicide.

The *curé* of Montreux, in Switzerland, ninety-six years old, still vigorous in mind and body, and able to preach. He had a twin-brother, also a preacher, and the exact likeness of himself. Sometimes strangers have beheld a white-haired, venerable clerical personage, nearly a century old; and, upon riding a few miles farther, have been astonished to meet again this white-haired, venerable, century-old personage.

When the body of Lord Mohun (killed in a duel) was carried home, bleeding, to his house, Lady Mohun was very angry because it was " flung upon the best bed."

A prophecy, somewhat in the style of Swift's about Partridge, but embracing various events and personages.

An incident that befell Dr. Harris, while a Junior at college. Being in great want of money to buy shirts or other necessaries, and not knowing how to obtain it, he set out on a walk from Cambridge to Boston. On the way he cut a stick, and, after walking a short distance, perceived that something had become attached to the end of it. It proved to be a gold ring, with the motto " God speed thee, friend."

Brobdingnag lay on the north-west coast of the American continent.

A gush of violets along a wood-path.

People with false hair and other artifices may be supposed to deceive Death himself, so that he does not know when their hour is come.

Bees are sometimes drowned (or suffocated) in the honey which they collect. So some writers are lost in their collected learning.

Advice of Lady Pepperell's father on her marriage,—never to work one moment after Saturday sunset,—never to lay down her knitting except in the middle of the needle,—always to rise with the sun,—to pass an hour daily with the housekeeper,—to visit every room daily from garret to cellar,—to attend herself to the brewing of beer and the baking of bread,—and to instruct every member of the family in their religious duties.

Service of plate, presented by the city of London to Sir William Pepperell, together with a table of solid silver. The table very narrow, but long; the articles of plate numerous, but of small dimensions,—the tureen not holding more than three pints. At the close of the Revolution, when the Pepperell and Sparhawk property was confiscated, this plate was sent to the grandson of Sir William, in London. It was so valuable, that Sheriff Moulton of old York, with six well-armed men, accompanied it to Boston. Pepperell's only daughter married Colonel Sparhawk, a fine gentleman of the day. Andrew Pepperell, the son, was rejected by a young lady (afterwards the mother of Mrs. General Knox), to whom he was on the point of marriage, as being addicted to low company and low pleasures. The lover, two days afterwards, in the streets of Portsmouth, was sun-struck, and fell down dead. Sir William had built an elegant house for his son and his intended wife; but after the death of the former he never entered it. He lost his cheerfulness and social qualities, and gave up intercourse with people, except on business. Very anxious to secure his property to his descendants by the provisions of his will, which was drawn up by Judge Sewall, then a young lawyer. Yet the judge lived to see two of Sir William's grandchildren so reduced that they were to have been numbered among the town's poor, and were only rescued from this fate by private charity.

The arms and crest of the Pepperell family were displayed over the door of every room in Sir William's house. In Colonel Sparhawk's house there were forty portraits, most of them in full length. The house built for Sir William's son was occupied as barracks during the Revolution, and much injured. A few years after the peace, it was blown down by a violent tempest, and finally no vestige of it was left, but there remained only a summer-house and the family tomb.

At Sir William's death, his mansion was hung with black, while the body lay in state for a week. All the Sparhawk portraits were covered with black crape, and the family pew was draped with black. Two oxen were roasted, and liquid hospitality dispensed in proportion.

Old lady's dress seventy or eighty years ago. Brown brocade gown, with a nice lawn handkerchief and apron,—short sleeves, with a little ruffle, just below the elbow,—black mittens,—a lawn cap, with rich lace border,—a black velvet hood on the back of the head, tied with black ribbon under the chin. She sat in an old-fashioned easy-chair, in a small, low parlour,—the wainscot painted entirely black, and the walls hung with a dark velvet paper.

A table, stationary ever since the house was built, extending the whole length of a room. One end was raised two steps higher than the rest. The Lady Ursula, an early Colonial heroine, was wont to dine at the upper end, while her servants sat below. This was in the kitchen. An old garden and summer-house, and roses, currant-bushes, and tulips, which Lady Ursula had brought from Grondale Abbey in Old England. Although a hundred and fifty years before, and though their roots were propagated all over the country, they were still flourishing in the original garden. This Lady Ursula was the daughter of Lord Thomas Cutts of Grondale Abbey in England. She had been in love with an officer named Fowler, who was supposed to have been slain in battle. After the death of her father and mother, Lady Ursula came to Kittery, bringing twenty men-servants and several women. After a time, a letter arrived from her lover, who was not killed, but merely a prisoner to the French. He announced his purpose to come to America, where he would arrive in October. A few days after the letter came, she went out in a low carriage to visit her work-people, and was blessing the food for their luncheon, when she fell dead, struck by an Indian tomahawk, as did all the rest save one. They were buried where the massacre took place, and a stone was erected, which (possibly) still remains. The lady's family had a grant from Sir Ferdinando

Gorges of the territory thereabout, and her brother had likewise come over and settled in the vicinity. I believe very little of this story. Long afterwards, at about the commencement of the Revolution, a descendant of Fowler came from England, and applied to the Judge of Probate to search the records for a will, supposed to have been made by Lady Ursula in favour of her lover as soon as she heard of his existence. In the meantime the estate had been sold to Colonel Whipple. No will could be found. (Lady Ursula was old Mrs. Cutts, widow of President Cutts.)

The mode of living of Lady Ursula's brother in Kittery. A drawbridge to the house, which was raised every evening, and lowered in the morning, for the labourers and the family to pass out. They kept thirty cows, a hundred sheep, and several horses. The house spacious,—one room large enough to contain forty or fifty guests. Two silver branches for candles,—the walls ornamented with paintings and needle-work. The floors were daily rubbed with wax, and shone like a mahogany table. A domestic chaplain, who said prayers every morning and evening in a small apartment called the chapel. Also a steward and butler. The family attended the Episcopal Church at Christmas, Easter, and Good Friday, and gave a grand entertainment once a year.

Madam Cutts, at the last of these entertainments, wore a black damask gown, and cuffs with double lace ruffles, velvet shoes, blue silk stockings, white and silver stomacher. The daughter and granddaughters in rich brocades and yellow satin. Old Major Cutts in brown velvet, laced with gold, and a large wig. The parson in his silk cassock, and his helpmate in brown damask. Old General Atkinson in scarlet velvet, and his wife and daughters in white damask. The Governor in black velvet, and his lady in crimson tabby trimmed with silver. The ladies wore bell-hoops, high-heeled shoes, paste buckles, silk stockings, and enormously high head-dresses, with lappets of Brussels lace hanging thence to the waist.

Among the eatables, a silver tub of the capacity of four gallons, holding a pyramid of pancakes powdered with white sugar.

The date assigned to all this about 1690.

What is the price of a day's labour in Lapland, where the sun never sets for six months?

Miss Asphyxia Davis!

A life, generally of a grave hue, may be said to be *embroidered* with occasional sports and fantasies.

A father confessor,—his reflections on character, and the contrast of the inward man with the outward, as he looks around on his congregation, all whose secret sins are known to him.

A person with an ice-cold hand,—his right hand, which people ever afterwards remember when once they have grasped it.

A stove possessed by a devil.

June 1*st*, 1842.—One of my chief amusements is to see the boys sail their miniature vessels on the Frog Pond. There is a great variety of shipping owned among the young people, and they appear to have a considerable knowledge of the art of managing vessels. There is a full-rigged man-of-war, with, I believe, every spar, rope, and sail, that sometimes makes its appearance; and, when on a voyage across the pond, it so identically resembles a great ship, except in size, that it has the effect of a picture. All its motions,—its tossing up and down on the small waves, and its sinking and rising in a calm swell, its heeling to the breeze,—the whole effect, in short, is that of a real ship at sea ; while, moreover, there is something that kindles the imagination more than the reality would do. If we see a real, great ship, the mind grasps and possesses, within its real clutch, all that there is of it ; while here the mimic ship is the representation of an ideal one, and so gives us a more imaginative pleasure. There are many schooners that ply to and fro on the pond, and pilot-boats, all perfectly rigged. I saw a race, the other day, between the ship above mentioned and a pilot-boat, in which the latter came off conqueror. The boys appear to be well acquainted with all the ropes and sails, and can call them by their nautical names. One of the owners of the vessels remains on one side of the pond, and the other on the opposite side, and so they send the little bark to and fro, like merchants of different countries, consigning their vessels to one another.

Generally, when any vessel is on the pond, there are full-grown spectators who look on with as much interest as the boys themselves. Towards sunset, this is especially the case : for then are seen young girls and their lovers ; mothers, with their little boys in hand ; school-girls, beating hoops round about, and occasionally running to the side of the pond; rough tars, or perhaps masters or young mates of vessels, who make remarks about the miniature shipping, and occasionally give professional advice to the navigators; visitors from the country; gloved and caned young gentlemen;—in short, everybody stops to take a look. In the meantime, dogs are continually plunging into the pond, and swimming about, with noses pointed upward, and snatching at floating chips; then, emerging, they shake themselves, scattering a horizontal shower on the clean gowns of ladies and trousers of gentlemen; then scamper to and fro on the grass, with joyous barks.

Some boys cast off lines of twine with pin-hooks, and perhaps pull out a horned-pout,—that being, I think, the only kind of fish that inhabits the Frog Pond.

The ship-of-war above mentioned is about three feet from stem to stern, or possibly a few inches more. This, if I mistake not, was the size of a ship-of-the-line in the navy of Lilliput.

Fancy pictures of familiar places which one has never been in, as the green-room of a theatre, &c.

The famous characters of history,—to imagine their

spirits now extant on earth, in the guise of various public or private personages.

The case quoted in Combe's Physiology of a young man of great talents and profound knowledge of chemistry, who had in view some new discovery of importance. In order to put his mind into the highest possible activity, he shut himself up for several successive days, and used various methods of excitement. He had a singing-girl, he drank spirits, smelled penetrating odours, sprinkled Cologne-water round the room, &c. &c. Eight days thus passed, when he was seized with a fit of frenzy which terminated in mania.

Flesh and Blood,—a firm of butchers.

Miss Polly Syllable,—a schoolmistress.

Mankind are earthen jugs with spirits in them.

A spendthrift,—in one sense he has his money's worth by the purchase of large lots of repentance and other dolorous commodities.

To symbolize moral or spiritual disease by disease

of the body; as thus,—when a person committed any sin, it might appear in some form on the body,—this to be wrought out.

"Shrieking fish," a strange idea of Leigh Hunt.

In my museum, all the ducal rings that have been thrown into the Adriatic.

An association of literary men in the other world, —or dialogues of the dead, or something of that kind.

Imaginary diseases to be cured by impossible remedies,—as a dose of the Grand Elixir in the yolk of a Phœnix's egg. The disease may be either moral or physical.

A physician for the cure of moral diseases.

To point out the moral slavery of one who deems himself a free man.

A stray leaf from the book of fate, picked up in the street.

Concord, August 5*th.*—A rainy day,— a rainy day.

I am commanded to take pen in hand, and I am therefore banished to the little ten-foot-square apartment misnamed my study; but perhaps the dismalness of the day and the dulness of my solitude will be the prominent characteristics of what I write. And what is there to write about? Happiness has no succession of events, because it is a part of eternity; and we have been living in eternity ever since we came to this old manse. Like Enoch, we seem to have been translated to the other state of being, without having passed through death. Our spirits must have flitted away unconsciously, and we can only perceive that we have cast off our mortal part by the more real and earnest life of our souls. Externally, our Paradise has very much the aspect of a pleasant old domicile on earth. This antique house,—for it looks antique, though it was created by Providence expressly for our use, and at the precise time when we wanted it,—stands behind a noble avenue of balm-of-Gilead trees; and when we chance to observe a passing traveller through the sunshine and the shadow of this long avenue, his figure appears too dim and remote to disturb the sense of blissful seclusion. Few, indeed, are the mortals who venture within our sacred precincts. George Prescott, who has not yet grown earthly enough, I suppose, to be debarred from occasional visits to Paradise, comes daily to bring three pints of milk from some ambrosial cow; occasionally, also, he makes an offering of mortal flowers. Mr. Emerson comes sometimes, and has been feasted on our nectar and ambrosia. Mr. Thoreau has twice listened to the music of the spheres, which, for our private convenience, we have packed into a musical box. E—— H——, who is much more at home among spirits than among fleshly bodies, came hither a few times merely to welcome us to the ethereal world ; but latterly she has vanished into some other region of infinite space. One rash mortal, on the second Sunday after our arrival, obtruded himself upon us in a gig. There have since been three or four callers, who preposterously think that the courtesies of the lower world are to be responded to by people whose home is in Paradise. I must not forget to mention that the butcher comes twice or thrice a week; and we have so far improved upon the custom of Adam and Eve, that we generally furnish forth our feasts with portions of some delicate calf or lamb, whose unspotted innocence entitles them to the happiness of becoming our sustenance. Would that I were permitted to record the celestial dainties that kind Heaven provided for us on the first day of our arrival! Never, surely, was such food heard of on earth,—at least, not by me. Well, the above-mentioned persons are nearly all that have entered into the hallowed shade of our avenue; except, indeed, a certain sinner who came to bargain for the grass in our orchard, and another who came with a new cistern. For it is one of the drawbacks upon our Eden that it contains no water fit either to drink or to bathe in; so that the showers have become, in good truth, a godsend. I wonder why Providence does not cause a clear, cold fountain to bubble up at our doorstep; methinks it would not be unreasonable to pray for such a favour. At present we are under the ridiculous necessity of sending to the outer world for water. Only imagine Adam trudging out of Paradise with a bucket in each hand, to get water to drink, or for Eve to bathe in! Intolerable! (though our stout handmaiden really fetches our water.) In other respects Providence has treated us pretty tolerably well; but here I shall expect something further to be done. Also, in the way of future favours, a kitten would be very acceptable. Animals (except, perhaps, a pig) seem never out of place, even in the most paradisiacal spheres. And, by the way, a young colt comes up our avenue, now and then, to crop the seldom-trodden herbage; and so does a company of cows, whose sweet breath well repays us for the food which they obtain. There are likewise a few hens, whose quiet cluck is heard pleasantly about the house. A black dog sometimes stands at the farther extremity of the avenue, and looks wistfully hitherward; but when I whistle to him, he puts his tail between his legs and trots away. Foolish dog! if he had more faith, he should have bones enough.

Saturday, August 6th.—Still a dull day, threatening rain, yet without energy of character enough to rain outright. However, yesterday there were showers enough to supply us well with their beneficent outpouring. As to the new cistern, it seems to be bewitched; for, while the spout pours into it like a cataract, it still remains almost empty. I wonder where Mr. Hosmer got it; perhaps from Tantalus, under the eaves of whose palace it must formerly have stood; for, like his drinking-cup in Hades, it has the property of filling itself for ever, and never being full.

After breakfast I took my fishing-rod, and went down through our orchard to the river-side; but as three or four boys were already in possession of the best spots along the shore, I did not fish. This river of ours is the most sluggish stream that I ever was acquainted with. I had spent three weeks by its side, and swam across it every day, before I could determine which way its current ran; and then I was compelled to decide the question by the testimony of others, and not by my own observation. Owing to this torpor of the stream, it has nowhere a bright, pebbly shore, nor is there so much as a narrow strip of glistening sand in any part of its course; but it slumbers along between broad meadows, or kisses the tangled grass of mowing-fields and pastures, or bathes the overhanging boughs of elder-bushes and other water-loving plants. Flags and rushes grow along its shallow margin. The yellow water-lily spreads its broad flat leaves upon its surface; and the fragrant white pond-lily occurs in many favoured spots,—generally selecting a situation just so far from the river's brink that it cannot be grasped except at the hazard of plunging in. But thanks be to the beautiful flower for growing at any rate. It is a marvel whence it derives its loveliness and perfume, sprouting as it does from the black mud over which the river sleeps, and from which the yellow lily likewise draws its unclean life and noisome odour. So it is with many people in this world: the same soil and circumstances may produce the good and beautiful, and the wicked and ugly. Some have the faculty of assimilating to themselves only what is evil, and so they become as noisome as the yellow water-lily. Some assimilate none but good influences, and their emblem is the fragrant and spotless pond-lily, whose very breath is a blessing to all the region round about. . . . Among the productions of the river's margin, I must not forget the pickerel-weed, which grows just on the edge of the water, and shoots up a long stalk crowned with a blue spire, from among large green leaves. Both the flower and the leaves look well in a vase with pond-lilies, and relieve the unvaried whiteness of the latter; and, being all alike children of the waters, they are perfectly in keeping with one another. . . .

I bathe once, and often twice, a day in our river; but one dip into the salt sea would be worth more than a whole week's soaking in such a lifeless tide. I have read of a river somewhere (whether it be in classic regions or among our Western Indians I know not), which seemed to dissolve and steal away the vigour of those who bathed in it. Perhaps our stream will be found to have this property. Its water, however, is pleasant in its immediate effect, being as soft as milk, and always warmer than the air. Its hue has a slight tinge of gold, and my limbs, when I behold them through its medium, look tawny. I am not aware that the inhabitants of Concord resemble their native river in any of their moral characteristics. Their forefathers, certainly, seem to have had the energy and impetus of a mountain torrent, rather than the torpor of this listless stream,—as it was proved by the blood with which they stained their river of Peace. It is said there are plenty of fish in it; but my most important captures hitherto have been a mud-turtle and an enormous eel. The former made his escape to his native element,—the latter we ate; and truly he had the taste of the whole river in his flesh, with a very prominent flavour of mud. On the whole, Concord River is no great favourite of mine; but I am glad to have any river at all so near at hand, it being just at the bottom of our orchard. Neither is it without a degree and kind of picturesqueness, both in its nearness and in the distance, when a blue gleam from its surface, among the green meadows and woods, seems like an open eye in Earth's countenance. Pleasant it is, too, to behold a little flat-bottomed skiff gliding over its bosom, which yields lazily to the stroke of the paddle, and allows the boat to go against its current almost as freely as with it. Pleasant, too, to watch an angler, as he strays along the brink, sometimes sheltering himself behind a tuft of bushes, and trailing his line along the water, in hopes to catch a pickerel. But, taking the river for all in all, I can find nothing more fit to compare it with than one of the half-torpid earthworms which I dig up for bait. The worm is sluggish, and so is the river,—the river is muddy, and so is the worm. You hardly know whether either of them be alive or dead; but still, in the course of time, they both manage to creep away. The best aspect of the Concord is when there is a north-western breeze curling its surface, in a bright, sunshiny day. It then assumes a vivacity not its own. Moonlight, also, gives it beauty, as it does to all scenery of earth or water.

Sunday, August 7th.—At sunset last evening I ascended the hill-top opposite our house; and, looking downward at the long extent of the river, it struck me that I had done it some injustice in my remarks. Perhaps, like other gentle and quiet characters, it will be better appreciated the longer I am acquainted with it. Certainly, as I beheld it then, it was one of the loveliest features in a scene of great rural beauty. It was visible through a course of two or three miles, sweeping in a semicircle round the hill on which I stood, and being the central line of a broad vale on either side. At a distance, it looked like a strip of sky set into the earth, which it so etherealized and idealized that it seemed akin to the upper regions. Nearer the base of the hill, I could discern the shadows of every tree and rock, imaged with a distinctness that made them even more charming than the reality; because, knowing them to be unsubstantial, they assumed the ideality which the soul always craves in the contemplation of earthly beauty. All the sky, too, and the rich clouds of sunset, were reflected in the peaceful bosom of the river; and surely, if its bosom can give back such an adequate reflection of heaven, it cannot be so gross and impure as I described it yesterday. Or, if so, it shall be a symbol to me that even a human breast, which may appear least spiritual in some aspects, may still have the capability of reflecting an infinite heaven in its depths, and therefore of enjoying it. It is a comfortable thought, that the smallest and most turbid mud-puddle can contain its own picture of heaven. Let us remember this, when we feel inclined to deny all spiritual life to some people, in whom, nevertheless, our Father may perhaps see the image of His face. This dull river has a deep religion of its own : so, let us trust, has the dullest human soul, though, perhaps, unconsciously.

The scenery of Concord, as I beheld it from the summit of the hill, has no very marked characteristics, but has a great deal of quiet beauty, in keeping with the river. There are broad and peaceful meadows, which, I think, are among the most satisfying objects in natural scenery. The heart reposes on them with a feeling that few things else can give, because almost all other objects are abrupt and clearly defined ; but a meadow stretches out like a small infinity, yet with a secure homeliness which we do not find either in an expanse of water or of air. The hills which border these meadows are wide swells of land, or long and gradual ridges, some of them densely covered with wood. The white village, at a distance on the left, appears to be embosomed among wooded hills. The verdure of the country is much more perfect than is usual at this season of the year, when the autumnal hue has generally made considerable progress over trees and grass. Last evening, after the copious showers of the preceding two days, it was worthy of early June, or, indeed, of a world just created. Had I not then been alone, I should have had a far deeper sense of beauty, for I should have looked through the medium of another spirit. Along the horizon there were masses of those deep clouds in which the fancy may see images of all things that ever existed or were dreamed of. Over our old manse, of which I could catch but a glimpse among its embowering trees, appeared the immensely gigantic figure of a hound, crouching down with head erect, as if keeping watchful guard while the master of the mansion was away. . . . How sweet it was to draw near my own home, after having lived homeless in the world so long! . . . With thoughts like these, I descended the hill, and clambered over the stone wall, and crossed the road, and passed up our avenue, while the quaint old house put on an aspect of welcome.

Monday, August 8th.—I wish I could give a description of our house, for it really has a character of its own, which is more than can be said of most edifices in these days. It is two storeys high, with a third storey of attic chambers in the gable-roof. When I first visited it, early in June, it looked pretty

much as it did during the old clergyman's lifetime,
showing all the dust and disarray that might be
supposed to have gathered about him in the course
of sixty years of occupancy. The rooms seemed
never to have been painted; at all events, the walls
and panels, as well as the huge cross-beams, had a
venerable and most dismal tinge of brown. The
furniture consisted of high-backed, short-legged, rheumatic chairs, small old tables, bedsteads with lofty
posts, stately chests of drawers, looking-glasses in
antique black frames, all of which were probably
fashionable in the days of Dr. Ripley's predecessor.
It required some energy of imagination to conceive
the idea of transforming this ancient edifice into a
comfortable modern residence. However, it has been
successfully accomplished. The old Doctor's sleeping apartment, which was the front room on the
ground-floor, we have converted into a parlour; and,
by the aid of cheerful paint and paper, a gladsome
carpet, pictures and engravings, new furniture, *bijou-
terie*, and a daily supply of flowers, it has become one
of the prettiest and pleasantest rooms in the whole
world. The shade of our departed host will never
haunt it; for its aspect has been changed as completely as the scenery of a theatre. Probably the

ghost gave one peep into it, uttered a groan, and vanished for ever. The opposite room has been metamorphosed into a store-room. Through the house, both in the first and second storey, runs a spacious hall or entry, occupying more space than is usually devoted to such a purpose in modern times. This feature contributes to give the whole house an airy, roomy, and convenient appearance; we can breathe the freer by the aid of the broad passageway. The front door of the hall looks up the stately avenue, which I have already mentioned; and the opposite door opens into the orchard, through which a path descends to the river. In the second storey we have at present fitted up three rooms,—one being our own chamber, and the opposite one a guest-chamber, which contains the most presentable of the old Doctor's ante-Revolutionary furniture. After all, the moderns have invented nothing better, as chamber furniture, than these chests of drawers, which stand on four slender legs, and rear an absolute tower of mahogany to the ceiling, the whole terminating in a fantastically carved summit. Such a venerable structure adorns our guest-chamber. In the rear of the house is the little room which I call my study, and which, in its day, has witnessed the intellectual labours of better students than myself. It contains, with some additions and alterations, the furniture of my bachelor-room in Boston; but there is a happier disposal of things now. There is a little vase of flowers on one of the bookcases, and a larger bronze vase of graceful ferns that surmounts the bureau. In size the room is just what it ought to be; for I never could compress my thoughts sufficiently to write in a very spacious room. It has three windows, two of which are shaded by a large and beautiful willow-tree, which sweeps against the overhanging eaves. On this side we have a view into the orchard, and, beyond, a glimpse of the river. The other window is the one from which Mr. Emerson, the predecessor of Dr. Ripley, beheld the first fight of the Revolution,— which he might well do, as the British troops were drawn up within a hundred yards of the house; and on looking forth just now, I could still perceive the western abutments of the old bridge, the passage of which was contested. The new monument is visible from base to summit.

Notwithstanding all we have done to modernize the old place, we seem scarcely to have disturbed its air of antiquity. It is evident that other wedded pairs have spent their honeymoons here, that children have been born here, and people have grown old and died in these rooms, although for our behoof the same apartments have consented to look cheerful once again. Then there are dark closets, and strange nooks and corners, where the ghosts of former occupants might hide themselves in the daytime, and stalk forth when night conceals all our sacrilegious improvements. We have seen no apparitions as yet; but we hear strange noises, especially in the kitchen, and last night, while sitting in the parlour, we heard a thumping and pounding as of somebody at work in my study. Nay, if I mistake not (for I was half asleep), there was a sound as of some person crumpling paper in his hand in our very bedchamber. This must have been old Dr. Ripley with one of his sermons. There is a whole chest of them in the garret; but he need have no apprehensions of our disturbing them. I never saw the old patriarch myself, which I regret, as I should have been glad to associate his venerable figure at ninety years of age with the house in which he dwelt.

Externally the house presents the same appearance as in the Doctor's day. It had once a coat of white paint; but the storms and sunshine of many years have almost obliterated it, and produced a sober, greyish hue, which entirely suits the antique form of the structure. To repaint its reverend face would be a real sacrilege. It would look like old Dr. Ripley in a brown wig. I hardly know why it is that our cheerful and lightsome repairs and improvements in the interior of the house seem to be in perfectly good taste, though the heavy old beams and high wainscoting of the walls speak of ages gone by. But so it is. The cheerful paper-hangings have the air of belonging to the old walls; and such modernisms as astral lamps, card-tables, gilded Cologne-bottles, silver taper-stands, and bronze and alabaster flower-vases, do not seem at all impertinent. It is thus that an aged man may keep his heart warm for new things and new friends, and often furnish himself anew with ideas; though it would not be graceful for him to attempt to suit his exterior to the passing fashions of the day.

August 9th.—Our orchard in its day has been a very productive and profitable one; and we were told that in one year it returned Dr. Ripley a hundred dollars, besides defraying the expense of repairing the house. It is now long past its prime: many of the trees are moss-grown, and have dead and rotten branches intermixed among the green and fruitful ones. And it may well be so; for I suppose some of the trees may have been set out by Mr. Emerson, who died in the first year of the Revolutionary war. Neither will the fruit, probably, bear comparison with the delicate productions of modern pomology. Most of the trees seem to have abundant burdens upon them; but they are homely russet apples, fit only for baking and cooking. (But we are yet to have practical experience of our fruit.) Justice Shallow's orchard, with its choice pippins and leather-coats, was doubtless much superior. Nevertheless, it pleases me to think of the good minister, walking in the shadows of these old, fantastically shaped apple-trees, here plucking some of the fruit to taste, there pruning away a too luxuriant branch, and all the while computing how many barrels may be filled, and how large a sum will be added to his stipend by their sale. And the same trees offer their fruit to me as freely as they did to him,—their old branches, like withered hands and arms, holding out apples of the same flavour as they held out to Dr. Ripley in his lifetime. Thus the trees, as living existences, form a peculiar link between the dead and us. My fancy has always found something very interesting in an orchard.

Apple-trees, and all fruit-trees, have a domestic character which brings them into relationship with man. They have lost, in a great measure, the wild nature of the forest-tree, and have grown humanized by receiving the care of man, and by contributing to his wants. They have become a part of the family; and their individual characters are as well understood and appreciated as those of the human members. One tree is harsh and crabbed, another mild; one is churlish and illiberal, another exhausts itself with its free-hearted bounties. Even the shapes of apple-trees have great individuality, into such strange postures do they put themselves, and thrust their contorted branches so grotesquely in all directions. And when they have stood around a house for many years, and held converse with successive dynasties of occupants, and gladdened their hearts so often in the fruitful autumn, then it would seem almost sacrilege to cut them down.

Besides the apple-trees, there are various other kinds of fruit in close vicinity to the house. When we first arrived, there were several trees of ripe cherries, but so sour that we allowed them to wither upon the branches. Two long rows of currant-bushes supplied us abundantly for nearly four weeks. There are a good many peach-trees, but all of an old date,—their branches rotten, gummy, and mossy,—and their fruit, I fear, will be of very inferior quality. They produce most abundantly, however,—the peaches being almost as numerous as the leaves; and even the sprouts and suckers from the roots of the old trees have fruit upon them. Then there are pear-trees of various kinds, and one or two quince-trees. On the whole, these fruit-trees, and the other items and adjuncts of the place, convey a very agreeable idea of the outward comfort in which the good old doctor must have spent his life. Everything seems to have fallen to his lot that could possibly be supposed to render the life of a country clergyman easy and prosperous. There is a barn, which probably used to be filled annually with his hay and other agricultural products. There are sheds, and a hen-house, and a pigeon-house, and an old stone pigsty, the open portion of which is overgrown with tall weeds, indicating that no grunter has recently occupied it. . . . I have serious thoughts of inducting a new incumbent in this part of the parsonage. It is our duty to support a pig, even if we have no design of feasting upon him; and, for my own part, I have a great sympathy and interest for the whole race of porkers, and should have much amusement in studying the character of a pig. Perhaps I might try to bring out his moral and intellectual nature, and cultivate his affections. A cat, too, and perhaps a dog, would be desirable additions to our household.

August 10*th.*—The natural taste of man for the original Adam's occupation is fast developing itself in me. I find that I am a good deal interested in our garden, although, as it was planted before we came here, I do not feel the same affection for the plants that I should if the seed had been sown by my own hands. It is something like nursing and educating another person's children. Still, it was a very pleasant moment when I gathered the first string-beans, which were the earliest esculent that the garden contributed to our table. And I love to watch the successive development of each new vegetable, and mark its daily growth, which always affects me with surprise. It is as if something were being created under my own inspection, and partly by my own aid. One day, perchance, I look at my bean-vines, and see only the green leaves clambering up the poles; again, to-morrow, I give a second glance, and there are the delicate blossoms; and a third day, on a somewhat closer observation, I discover the tender young beans, hiding among the foliage. Then, each morning, I watch the swelling of the pods, and calculate how soon they will be ready to yield their treasures. All this gives a pleasure and an ideality, hitherto unthought of, to the business of providing sustenance for my family. I suppose Adam felt it in Paradise; and, of merely and exclusively earthly enjoyments, there are few purer and more harmless to be experienced. Speaking of beans, by the way, they are a classical food, and their culture must have been the occupation of many ancient sages and heroes. Summer-squashes are a very pleasant vegetable to be acquainted with. They grow in the forms of urns and vases,— some shallow, others deeper, and all with a beautifully scalloped edge. Almost any squash in our garden might be copied by a sculptor, and would look lovely in marble, or in china; and, if I could afford it, I would have exact imitations of the real vegetable as portions of my dining-service. They would be very appropriate dishes for holding garden-vegetables. Besides the summer-squashes, we have the crook-necked winter-squash, which I always delight to look at, when it turns up its big rotundity to ripen in the autumn sun. Except a pumpkin, there is no vegetable production that imparts such an idea of warmth and comfort to the beholder. Our own crop, however, does not promise to be very abundant; for the leaves formed such a superfluous shade over the young blossoms that most of them dropped off without producing the germ of fruit. Yesterday and to-day I have cut off an immense number of leaves, and have thus given the remaining blossoms a chance to profit by the air and sunshine; but the season is too far advanced, I am afraid, for the squashes to attain any great bulk, and grow yellow in the sun. We have musk-melons and watermelons, which promise to supply us with as many as we can eat. After all, the greatest interest of these vegetables does not seem to consist in their being articles of food. It is rather that we love to see something born into the world; and when a great squash or melon is produced, it is a large and tangible existence, which the imagination can seize hold of and rejoice in. I love, also, to see my own works contributing to the life and well-being of animate nature. It is pleasant to have the bees come and suck honey out of my squash-blossoms, though, when they have laden themselves, they fly away to some unknown hive, which will give me back nothing in return for what my garden has given them. But there is much more honey in the world, and so I am content. Indian corn, in the prime and glory of its verdure, is a very beautiful vegetable, both considered in the separate plant, and in a mass in a broad field, rustling and waving, and surging up and down in the breeze and sunshine of a summer afternoon. We have as many as fifty hills, I should think, which will give us an abundant supply. Pray Heaven that we may be able to eat it all! for it is not pleasant to think that anything which Nature has been at the pains to produce should be thrown away. But the hens will be glad of our superfluity, and so will the pigs, though we have neither hens nor pigs of our own. But hens we must certainly keep. There is something very sociable and quiet, and soothing too, in their soliloquies and converse among themselves; and, in an idle and half-meditative mood, it is very pleasant to watch a party of hens picking up their daily subsistence, with a gallant chanticleer in the midst of them. Milton had evidently contemplated such a picture with delight.

I find that I have not given a very complete idea of our garden, although it certainly deserves an ample record in this chronicle, since my labours in it are the only present labours of my life. Besides what I have mentioned, we have cucumber-vines, which to-day yielded us the first cucumber of the season, a bed of beets, and another of carrots, and another of parsnips and turnips, none of which promise us a very abundant harvest. In truth, the soil is worn out, and, moreover, received very little manure this season. Also, we have cabbages in superfluous abundance, inasmuch as we neither of us have the least affection for them; and it would be unreasonable to expect Sarah, the cook, to eat fifty head of cabbages. Tomatoes, too, we shall have by and by. At our first arrival, we found green pease ready for gathering, and these, instead of the string-beans, were the first offering of the garden to our board.

Saturday, August 13*th*.—My life, at this time, is more like that of a boy, externally, than it has been since I was really a boy. It is usually supposed that the cares of life come with matrimony; but I seem to have cast off all care, and live on with as much easy trust in Providence as Adam could possibly haav felt before he had learned that there was a world beyond Paradise. My chief anxiety consists in watching the prosperity of my vegetables, in observing how they are affected by the rain or sunshine, in lamenting the blight of one squash and rejoicing at the luxurious growth of another. It is as if the original relation between man and Nature were restored in my case, and as if I were to look exclusively to her for the support of my Eve and myself,—to trust to her for food and clothing, and all things needful, with the full assurance that she would not fail me. The fight with the world,—the struggle of a man among men,—the agony of the universal effort to wrench the means of living from a host of greedy competitors,—all this seems like a dream to me. My business is merely to live and to enjoy; and whatever is essential to life and enjoyment will come as naturally as the dew from heaven. This is, practically at least, my faith. And so I awake in the morning with a boyish thoughtlessness as to how the outgoings of the day are to be provided for, and its incomings rendered certain. After breakfast, I go forth into my garden, and gather whatever the bountiful Mother has made fit for our present sustenance; and of late days she generally gives me two squashes and a cucumber, and promises me green corn and shell-beans very soon. Then I pass down through our orchard to the river-side, and ramble along its margin in search of flowers. Usually I discern a fragrant white lily here and there along the shore, growing, with sweet prudishness, beyond the grasp of mortal arm. But it does not escape me so. I know what is its fitting destiny better than the silly flower knows for itself; so I wade in, heedless of wet trousers, and seize the shy lily by its slender stem. Thus I make prize of five or six, which are as many as usually blossom within my reach in a single morning;—some of them partially worm-eaten or blighted, like virgins with an eating sorrow at the heart; others as fair and perfect as Nature's own idea was, when she first imagined this lovely flower. A perfect pond-lily is the most satisfactory of flowers. Besides these, I gather whatever else of beautiful chances to be growing in the moist soil by the river-side,—an amphibious tribe, yet with more richness and grace than the wild-flowers of the deep and dry woodlands and hedgerows,—sometimes the white arrow-head, always the blue spires and broad green leaves of the pickerel-flower, which contrast and harmonize so well with the white lilies. For the last two or three days I have found scattered stalks of the cardinal-flower, the gorgeous scarlet of which it is a joy even to remember. The world is made brighter and sunnier by flowers of such a hue. Even perfume, which otherwise is the soul and spirit of a flower, may be spared when it arrays itself in this scarlet glory. It is a flower of thought and feeling, too; it seems to have its roots deep down in the hearts of those who gaze at it. Other bright flowers sometimes impress me as wanting sentiment; but it is not so with this.

Well, having made up my bunch of flowers, I return home with them. . . . . Then I ascend to my study, and generally read, or perchance scribble in this journal, and otherwise suffer Time to loiter onward at his own pleasure, till the dinner-hour. In pleasant days, the chief event of the afternoon, and the happiest one of the day, is our walk. . . . So comes the night; and I look back upon a day spent in what the world would call idleness, and for which I myself can suggest no more appropriate epithet, but which, nevertheless, I cannot feel to have been spent amiss. True, it might be a sin and shame, in such a world as ours, to spend a lifetime in this manner; but for a few summer weeks it is good to live as if this world were heaven. And so it is, and so it shall be, although, in a little while, a flitting shadow of earthly care and toil will mingle itself with our realities.

Monday, August 15*th.*—George Hillard and his wife arrived from Boston in the dusk of Saturday evening, to spend Sunday with us. It was a pleasant sensation, when the coach rumbled up our avenue, and wheeled round at the door; for I felt that I was regarded as a man with a household,—a man having a tangible existence and locality in the world,—when friends came to avail themselves of our hospitality. It was a sort of acknowledgment and reception of us into the corps of married people,—a sanction by no means essential to our peace and well-being, but yet agreeable enough to receive. So we welcomed them cordially at the door, and ushered them into our parlour, and soon into the supper-room. . . . The night flitted over us all, and passed away, and up rose a grey and sullen morning, ... and we had a splendid breakfast of flapjacks, or slapjacks, and whortleberries, which I gathered on a neighbouring hill, and perch, bream, and pout, which I hooked out of the river the evening before. About nine o'clock, Hillard and I set out for a walk to Walden Pond, calling by the way at Mr. Emerson's, to obtain his guidance or directions, and he accompanied us in his own illustrious person. We turned aside a little from our way, to visit Mr. ——, a yeoman, of whose homely and self-acquired wisdom Mr. Emerson has a very high opinion. We found him walking in his fields, a short and stalwart and sturdy personage of middle age, with a face of shrewd and kind expression, and manners of natural courtesy. He had a very free flow of talk; for, with a little induction from Mr. Emerson, he began to discourse about the state of the nation, agriculture, and business in general, uttering thoughts that had come to him at the plough, and which had a sort of flavour of the fresh earth about them. His views were sensible and characteristic, and had grown in the soil where we found them; .... and he is certainly a man of intellectual and moral substance, a sturdy fact, a reality, something to be felt and touched, whose ideas seem to be dug out of his mind as he digs potatoes, beets, carrots, and turnips out of the ground.

After leaving Mr. ——, we proceeded through wood paths to Walden Pond, picking blackberries of enormous size along the way. The pond itself was beautiful and refreshing to my soul, after such long and exclusive familiarity with our tawny and sluggish river. It lies embosomed among wooded hills,—it is not very extensive, but large enough for waves to dance upon its surface, and to look like a piece of blue firmament, earth-encircled. The shore has a narrow, pebbly strand, which it was worth a day's journey to look at, for the sake of the contrast between it and the weedy, oozy margin of the river. Farther within its depths, you perceive a bottom of pure white sand, sparkling through the transparent water, which, methought, was the very purest liquid in the world. After Mr. Emerson left us, Hillard and I bathed in the pond, and it does really seem as if my spirit, as well as corporeal person, were refreshed by that bath. A good deal of mud and river slime had accumulated on my soul; but these bright waters washed them all away.

We returned home in due season for dinner. . . . To my misfortune, however, a box of Mediterranean wine proved to have undergone the acetous fermentation; so that the splendour of the festival suffered some diminution. Nevertheless, we ate our dinner with a good appetite, and afterwards went universally to take our several siestas. Meantime there came a shower, which so besprinkled the grass and shrubbery as to make it rather wet for our after-tea ramble. The chief result of the walk was the bringing home of an immense burden of the trailing clematis-vine, now just in blossom, and with which all our flower-stands and vases are this morning decorated. On our return, we found Mr. and Mrs. S——, and E. H——, who shortly took their leave, and we sat up late, telling ghost-stories. This morning, at seven, our friends left us. We were both pleased with the visit, and so, I think, were our guests.

*   *   *   *   *

Monday, August 22nd.—I took a walk through the woods yesterday afternoon, to Mr. Emerson's, with a book which Margaret Fuller had left, after a call on Saturday eve. I missed the nearest way, and wandered into a very secluded portion of the forest; for forest it might justly be called, so dense and sombre was the shade of oaks and pines. Once I wandered into a tract so overgrown with bushes and underbrush that I could scarcely force a passage through. Nothing is more annoying than a walk of this kind, where one is tormented by an innumerable host of petty impediments. It incenses and depresses me at the same time. Always when I flounder into the midst of bushes, which cross and intertwine themselves about my legs, and brush my face, and seize hold of my clothes, with their multitudinous grip,— always, in such a difficulty, I feel as if it were almost as well to lie down and die in rage and despair as to go one step farther. It is laughable, after I have got out of the moil, to think how miserably it affected me for the moment; but I had better learn patience betimes, for there are many such bushy tracts in this vicinity, on the margins of meadows, and my walks will often lead me into them. Escaping from the bushes, I soon came to an open space among the woods,—a very lovely spot, with the tall old trees standing around as quietly as if no one had intruded there throughout the whole summer. A company of crows were holding their Sabbath on their summits. Apparently they felt themselves injured or insulted by my presence; for, with one consent they began to caw! caw! caw! and, launching themselves sullenly on the air, took flight to some securer solitude. Mine, probably, was the first human shape that they had seen all day long,—at least, if they had been stationary in that spot; but perhaps they had winged their way over miles and miles of country, had breakfasted on the summit of Graylock, and dined at the base of Wachusett, and were merely come to sup and sleep among the quiet woods of Concord. But it was my impression at the time, that they had sat still and silent on the tops of the trees all through the Sabbath day, and I felt like one who should unawares disturb an assembly of worshippers. A crow, however, has no real pretensions to religion, in spite of his gravity of mien and black attire. Crows are certainly thieves, and probably infidels. Nevertheless, their voices yesterday were in admirable accordance with the influences of the quiet, sunny, warm, yet autumnal afternoon. They were so far above my head that their loud clamour added to the quiet of the scene, instead of disturbing it. There was no other sound, except the song of the cricket, which is but an audible stillness; for, though it be very loud and heard afar, yet the mind does not take note of it as a sound, so entirely does it mingle and lose its individuality among the other characteristics of coming autumn. Alas for the summer! The grass is still verdant on the hills and in the valleys; the foliage of the trees is as dense as ever, and as green; the flowers are abundant along the margin of the river, and in the hedgerows, and deep among the woods; the days, too, are as fervid as they were a month ago; and yet in every breath of wind and in every beam of sunshine there is an autumnal influence. I know not how to describe it. Methinks there is a sort of coolness amid all the heat, and a mildness in the brightest of the sunshine. A breeze cannot stir, without thrilling me with the breath of autumn, and I behold its pensive glory in the far golden gleams among the long shadows of the trees. The flowers, even the brightest of them,— the golden-rod and the gorgeous cardinals,—the most glorious flowers of the year,—have this gentle sadness amid their pomp. Pensive autumn is expressed in the glow of every one of them. I have felt this influence earlier in some years than in others. Sometimes autumn may be perceived even in the early days of July. There is no other feeling like that caused by this faint, doubtful, yet real perception, or rather prophecy, of the year's decay, so deliciously sweet and sad at the same time.

After leaving the book at Mr. Emerson's, I returned through the woods, and, entering Sleepy Hollow, I perceived a lady reclining near the path which bends along its verge. It was Margaret herself. She had been there the whole afternoon, meditating or reading; for she had a book in her hand, with some strange title, which I did not understand, and have forgotten. She said that nobody had broken her solitude, and was just giving utterance to a theory that no inhabitant of Concord ever visited Sleepy Hollow, when we saw a group of people entering the sacred precincts. Most of them followed a path which led them away from us; but an old man passed near us, and smiled to see Margaret reclining on the ground, and me sitting by her side. He made some remark about the beauty of the afternoon, and withdrew himself into the shadow of the wood. Then we talked about autumn, and about the pleasures of being lost in the woods, and about the crows, whose voices Margaret had heard; and about the experiences of early childhood, whose influence remains upon the character after the recollection of them has passed away; and about the sight of mountains from a distance, and the view from their summits; and about other matters of high and low philosophy. In the midst of our talk, we heard footsteps above us, on the high bank; and while the person was still hidden among the trees, he called to Margaret, of whom he had gotten a glimpse. Then he emerged from the green shade, and behold! it was Mr. Emerson. He appeared to have had a pleasant time, for he said that there were Muses in the woods to-day, and whispers to be heard in the breezes. It being now nearly six o'clock we separated,—Margaret and Mr. Emerson towards his home, and I towards mine. . .

Last evening there was the most beautiful moonlight that ever hallowed this earthly world; and when

I went to bathe in the river, which was as calm as death, it seemed like plunging down into the sky. But I had rather be on earth than even in the seventh heaven, just now.

Wednesday, August 24th.—I left home at five o'clock this morning to catch some fish for breakfast. I shook our summer apple-tree, and ate the golden apple which fell from it. Methinks these early apples, which come as a golden promise before the treasures of autumnal fruit, are almost more delicious than anything that comes afterwards. We have but one such tree in our orchard; but it supplies us with a daily abundance, and probably will do so for at least a week to come. Meantime other trees begin to cast their ripening windfalls upon the grass; and when I taste them, and perceive their mellowed flavour and blackening seeds, I feel somewhat overwhelmed with the impending bounties of Providence. I suppose Adam, in Paradise, did not like to see his fruits decaying on the ground, after he had watched them through the sunny days of the world's first summer. However, insects, at the worst, will hold a festival upon them, so that they will not be thrown away in the great scheme of Nature. Moreover, I have one advantage over the primeval Adam, inasmuch as there is a chance of disposing of my superfluous fruits among people who inhabit no Paradise of their own.

Passing a little way down along the river-side, I threw in my line, and soon drew out one of the smallest possible of fishes. It seemed to be a pretty good morning for the angler,—an autumnal coolness in the air, a clear sky, but with a fog across the lowlands and on the surface of the river, which a gentle breeze sometimes condensed into wreaths. At first I could barely discern the opposite shore of the river; but, as the sun arose, the vapours gradually dispersed, till only a warm, smoky tint was left along the water's surface. The farm-houses across the river made their appearance out of the dusky cloud; the voices of boys were heard, shouting to the cattle as they drove them to the pastures; a man whetted his scythe, and set to work in a neighbouring meadow. Meantime, I continued to stand on the oozy margin of the stream, beguiling the little fish; and though the scaly inhabitants of our river partake somewhat of the character of their native element, and are but sluggish biters, still I contrived to pull out not far from two dozen. They were all bream, a broad, flat, almost circular fish, shaped a good deal like a flounder, but swimming on their edges, instead of on their sides. As far as mere pleasure is concerned, it is hardly worth while to fish in our river, it is so much like angling in a mud-puddle; and one does not attach the idea of freshness and purity to the fishes, as we do to those which inhabit swift, transparent streams, or haunt the shores of the great briny deep. Standing on the weedy margin, and throwing the line over the elder-bushes that dip into the water, it seems as if we could catch nothing but frogs and mud-turtles, or reptiles akin to them. And even when a fish of reputable aspect is drawn out, one feels a shyness about touching him. As to our river, its character was admirably expressed last night by some one who said "it was too lazy to keep itself clean." I might write pages and pages, and only obscure the impression which this brief sentence conveys. Nevertheless, we made bold to eat some of my fish for breakfast, and found them very savoury; and the rest shall meet with due entertainment at dinner, together with some shell-beans, green corn, and cucumbers from our garden; so this day's food comes directly and entirely from beneficent Nature, without the intervention of any third person between her and us.

Saturday, August 27th.—A peach-tree, which grows beside our house and brushes against the window, is so burdened with fruit that I have had to prop it up. I never saw more splendid peaches in appearance,—great round crimson-cheeked beauties, clustering all over the tree. A pear-tree, likewise, is maturing a generous burden of small, sweet fruit, which will require to be eaten at about the same time as the peaches. There is something pleasantly annoying in this superfluous abundance; it is like standing under a tree of ripe apples, and giving it a shake, with the intention of bringing down a single one, when, behold, a dozen come thumping about our ears. But the idea of the infinite generosity and exhaustless bounty of our Mother Nature is well worth attaining; and I never had it so vividly as now, when I find myself, with the few mouths which I am to feed, the sole inheritor of the old clergyman's wealth of fruits. His children, his friends in the village, and the clerical guests who came to preach in his pulpit, were all wont to eat and be filled from these trees. Now, all these hearty old people have passed away, and in their stead is a solitary pair, whose appetites are more than satisfied with the windfalls which the trees throw down at their feet. Howbeit, we shall have now and then a guest to keep our peaches and pears from decaying.

G. B——, my old fellow-labourer at the community at Brook Farm, called on me last evening, and dined here to-day. He had been cultivating vegetables at Plymouth this summer, and selling them in the market. What a singular mode of life for a man of education and refinement,—to spend his days in hard and earnest bodily toil, and then to convey the products of his labour, in a wheelbarrow, to the public market, and there retail them out,—a peck of peas or beans, a bunch of turnips, a squash, a dozen ears of green corn! Few men, without some eccentricity of character, would have the moral strength to do this; and it is very striking to find such strength combined with the utmost gentleness, and an uncommon regularity of nature. Occasionally he returns for a day or two to resume his place among scholars and idle people, as, for instance, the present week, when he has thrown aside his spade and hoe to attend the Commencement at Cambridge. He is a rare man,—a perfect original, yet without any one salient point; a character to be felt and understood, but almost impossible to describe: for, should you seize upon any characteristic, it would inevitably be altered and distorted in the process of writing it down.

Our few remaining days of summer have been latterly grievously darkened with clouds. To-day there has been an hour or two of hot sunshine; but the sun rose amid cloud and mist, and before he could dry up the moisture of last night's shower upon the trees and grass, the clouds have gathered between him and us again. This afternoon the thunder rumbles in the distance, and I believe a few drops of rain have fallen; but the weight of the shower has burst elsewhere, leaving us nothing but its sullen gloom. There is a muggy warmth in the atmosphere, which takes all the spring and vivacity out of the mind and body.

Sunday, August 28*th.*—Still another rainy day,— the heaviest rain, I believe, that has fallen since we came to Concord (not two months ago). There never was a more sombre aspect of all external nature. I gaze from the open window of my study somewhat disconsolately, and observe the great willow-tree which shades the house, and which has caught and retained a whole cataract of rain among its leaves and boughs; and all the fruit-trees, too, are dripping continually, even in the brief intervals when the clouds give us a respite. If shaken to bring down the fruit, they will discharge a shower upon the head of him who stands beneath. The rain is warm, coming from some southern region; but the willow attests that it is an autumnal spell of weather, by scattering down no infrequent multitude of yellow leaves, which rest upon the sloping roof of the house, and strew the gravel-path and the grass. The other trees do not yet shed their leaves, though in some of them a lighter tint of verdure, tending towards yellow, is perceptible. All day long we hear the water drip, drip, dripping, splash, splash, splashing, from the eaves, and babbling and foaming into the tubs, which have been set out to receive it. The old unpainted shingles and boards of the mansion and out-houses are black with the moisture which they have imbibed. Looking at the river, we perceive that its usually smooth and mirrored surface is blurred by the infinity of rain-drops; the whole landscape—grass, trees, and houses—has a completely water-soaked aspect, as if the earth were wet through. The wooded hill, about a mile distant, whither we went to gather whortleberries, has a mist upon its summit, as if the demon of the rain were enthroned there; and if we look to the sky, it seems as if all the water that had been poured down upon us were as nothing to what is to come. Once in a while, indeed, there is a gleam of sky along the horizon, or a half-cheerful, half-sullen lighting up of the atmosphere; the raindrops cease to patter down, except when the trees shake off a gentle shower; but soon we hear the broad, quiet, slow and sure recommencement of the rain. The river, if I mistake not, has risen considerably during the day, and its current will acquire some degree of energy.

In this sombre weather, when some mortals almost forget that there ever was any golden sunshine, or ever will be any hereafter, others seem absolutely to radiate it from their own hearts and minds. The gloom cannot pervade them; they conquer it, and drive it quite out of their sphere, and create a moral rainbow of hope upon the blackest cloud. As for myself, I am little other than a cloud at such seasons, but such persons contrive to make me a sunny one, shining all through me. And thus, even without the support of a stated occupation, I survive these sullen days and am happy.

This morning we read the Sermon on the Mount. In the course of the forenoon, the rain abated for a season, and I went out and gathered some corn and summer-squashes, and picked up the windfalls of apples and pears and peaches. Wet, wet, wet,—

everything was wet; the blades of the corn-stalks moistened me; the wet grass soaked my boots quite through; the trees threw their reserved showers upon my head; and soon the remorseless rain began anew, and drove me into the house. When shall we be able to walk again to the far hills, and plunge into the deep woods, and gather more cardinals along the river's margin? The track along which we trod is probably under water now. How inhospitable Nature is during a rain! In the fervid heat of sunny days, she still retains some degree of mercy for us; she has shady spots, whither the sun cannot come; but she provides no shelter against her storms. It makes one shiver to think how dripping with wet are those deep, umbrageous nooks, those overshadowed banks, where we find such enjoyment during sultry afternoons. And what becomes of the birds in such a soaking rain as this? Is hope and an instinctive faith so mixed up with their nature that they can be cheered by the thought that the sunshine will return? or do they think, as I almost do, that there is to be no sunshine any more? Very disconsolate must they be among the dripping leaves; and when a single summer makes so important a portion of their lives, it seems hard that so much of it should be dissolved in rain. I, likewise, am greedy of the summer days for my own sake; the life of man does not contain so many of them that one can be spared without regret.

Tuesday, August 30th.—I was promised, in the midst of Sunday's rain, that Monday should be fair, and behold! the sun came back to us, and brought one of the most perfect days ever made since Adam was driven out of Paradise. By the by, was there ever any rain in Paradise? If so, how comfortless must Eve's bower have been! and what a wretched and rheumatic time must they have had on their bed of wet roses! It makes me shiver to think of it. Well, it seemed as if the world was newly created yesterday morning, and I beheld its birth; for I had risen before the sun was over the hill, and had gone forth to fish. How instantaneously did all dreariness and heaviness of the earth's spirit flit away before one smile of the beneficent sun! This proves that all gloom is but a dream and a shadow, and that cheerfulness is the real truth. It requires many clouds, long brooding over us, to make us sad, but one gleam of sunshine always suffices to cheer up the landscape. The banks of the river actually laughed when the sunshine fell upon them; and the river itself was alive and cheerful, and, by way of fun and amusement, it had swept away many wreaths of meadow-hay, and old, rotten branches of trees, and all such trumpery. These matters came floating downwards, whirling round and round in the eddies, or hastening onward in the main current; and many of them, before this time, have probably been carried into the Merrimack, and will be borne onward to the sea. The spots where I stood to fish, on my preceding excursion, were now under water; and the tops of many of the bushes, along the river's margin, barely emerged from the stream. Large spaces of meadow are overflowed.

There was a north-west wind throughout the day; and as many clouds, the remnants of departed gloom, were scattered about the sky, the breeze was continually blowing them across the sun. For the most part, they were gone again in a moment; but sometimes the shadow remained long enough to make me dread a return of sulky weather. Then would come the burst of sunshine, making me feel as if a rainy day were henceforth an impossibility. . . . .

In the afternoon Mr. Emerson called, bringing Mr. ——. He is a good sort of humdrum parson enough, and well fitted to increase the stock of manuscript sermons, of which there must be a fearful quantity in the world. Mr. ——, however, is probably one of the best and most useful of his class, because no suspicion of the necessity of his profession, constituted as it now is, to mankind, and of his own usefulness and success in it, has hitherto disturbed him; and therefore he labours with faith and confidence, as ministers did a hundred years ago.

After the visitors were gone, I sat at the gallery window, looking down the avenue; and soon there appeared an elderly woman,—a homely, decent old matron, dressed in a dark gown, and with what seemed a manuscript book under her arm. The wind sported with her gown, and blew her veil across her face, and seemed to make game of her, though on a nearer view she looked like a sad old creature, with a pale, thin countenance, and somewhat of a wild and wandering expression. She had a singular gait, reeling, as it were, and yet not quite reeling, from one side of the path to the other; going onward as if it were not much matter whether she went straight or crooked. Such were my observations as she approached through the scattered sunshine and shade of our long avenue, until, reaching the door, she gave a knock, and inquired for the lady of the house. Her manuscript contained a certificate, stating that the old woman was a widow from a foreign land, who had recently lost her son, and was now utterly destitute of friends and kindred, and without means of support. Appended to the certificate there was a list of names of people who had bestowed charity on her, with the amounts of their several donations,— none, as I recollect, higher than twenty-five cents. Here is a strange life, and a character fit for romance and poetry. All the early part of her life, I suppose, and much of her widowhood, were spent in the quiet of a home, with kinsfolk around her, and children, and the life-long gossiping acquaintances that some women always create about them. But in her decline she has wandered away from all these, and from her native country itself, and is a vagrant, yet with something of the homeliness and decency of aspect belonging to one who has been a wife and mother, and has had a roof of her own above her head,—and, with all this, a wildness proper to her present life. I have a liking for vagrants of all sorts, and never, that I know of, refused my mite to a wandering beggar, when I had anything in my own pocket. There is so much wretchedness in the world, that we may safely take the word of any mortal professing to need our assistance ; and, even should we be deceived, still the good to ourselves resulting from a kind act is worth more than the trifle by which we purchase it. It is desirable, I think, that such persons should be permitted to roam through our land of plenty, scattering the seeds of tenderness and charity, as birds of passage bear the seeds of precious plants from land to land, without even dreaming of the office which they perform.

Thursday, September 1st.—Mr. Thoreau dined with us yesterday. . . . He is a keen and delicate observer of nature,—a genuine observer,—which, I suspect, is almost as rare a character as even an original poet ; and Nature, in return for his love, seems to adopt him as her especial child, and shows him secrets which few others are allowed to witness. He is familiar with beast, fish, fowl, and reptile, and has strange stories to tell of adventures and friendly passages with these lower brethren of mortality. Herb and flower, likewise, wherever they grow, whether in garden or wild-wood, are his familiar friends. He is also on intimate terms with the clouds, and can tell the portents of storms. It is a characteristic trait, that he has a great regard for the memory of the

Indian tribes, whose wild life would have suited him so well; and, strange to say, he seldom walks over a ploughed field without picking up an arrow-point, spear-head, or other relic of the red man, as if their spirits willed him to be the inheritor of their simple wealth.

With all this he has more than a tincture of literature, a deep and true taste for poetry, especially for the elder poets, and he is a good writer,—at least he has written a good article, a rambling disquisition on Natural History, in the last *Dial*, which, he says, was chiefly made up from journals of his own observations. Methinks this article gives a very fair image of his mind and character,—so true, innate, and literal in observation, yet giving the spirit as well as letter of what he sees, even as a lake reflects its wooded banks, showing every leaf, yet giving the wild beauty of the whole scene. Then there are in the article passages of cloudy and dreamy metaphysics, and also passages where his thoughts seem to measure and attune themselves into spontaneous verse, as they rightfully may, since there is real poetry in them. There is a basis of good sense and of moral truth, too, throughout the article, which also is a reflection of his character; for he is not unwise to think and feel, and I find him a healthy and wholesome man to know.

After dinner (at which we cut the first watermelon and musk-melon that our garden has grown), Mr. Thoreau and I walked up the bank of the river, and at a certain point he shouted for his boat. Forthwith a young man paddled it across, and Mr. Thoreau and I voyaged farther up the stream, which soon became more beautiful than any picture, with its dark and quiet sheet of water, half shaded, half sunny, between high and wooded banks. The late rains have swollen the stream so much that many trees are standing up to their knees, as it were, in the water, and boughs, which lately swung high in air, now dip and drink deep of the passing wave. As to the poor cardinals which glowed upon the bank a few days since, I could see only a few of their scarlet hats peeping above the tide. Mr. Thoreau managed the boat so perfectly, either with two paddles or with one, that it seemed instinct with his own will, and to require no physical effort to guide it. He said that, when some Indians visited Concord a few years ago, he found that he had acquired, without a teacher, their precise method of propelling and steering a canoe. Nevertheless, he was desirous of selling the boat of which he was so fit a pilot, and which was built by his own hands; so I agreed to take it, and accordingly became possessor of the "Musketaquid." I wish I could acquire the aquatic skill of the original owner.

September 2nd.—Yesterday afternoon Mr. Thoreau arrived with the boat. The adjacent meadow being overflowed by the rise of the stream, he had rowed directly to the foot of the orchard, and landed at the bars, after floating over forty or fifty yards of water where people were lately making hay. I entered the boat with him, in order to have the benefit of a lesson in rowing and paddling. . . . I managed, indeed, to propel the boat by rowing with two oars, but the use of the single paddle is quite beyond my present skill. Mr. Thoreau had assured me that it was only necessary to will the boat to go in any particular direction, and she would immediately take that course, as if imbued with the spirit of the steersman. It may be so with him, but it is certainly not so with me. The boat seemed to be bewitched, and turned its head to every point of the compass except the right one. He then took the paddle himself, and, though I could observe nothing peculiar in his management of it, the "Musketaquid" immediately became as docile as a trained steed. I suspect that she has not yet transferred her affections from her old master to her new one. By and by, when we are better acquainted, she will grow more tractable. . . . We propose to change her name from "Musketaquid" (the Indian name of the Concord river, meaning the river of meadows,) to the "Pond-Lily," which will be very beautiful and appropriate, as, during the summer season, she will bring home many a cargo of pond-lilies from along the river's weedy shore. It is not very likely that I shall make such long voyages in her as Mr. Thoreau has made. He once followed our river down to the Merrimack, and thence, I believe, to Newburyport, in this little craft.

In the evening, —— —— called to see us, wishing to talk with me about a Boston periodical, of which he had heard that I was to be editor, and to which he desired to contribute. He is an odd and clever young man, with nothing very peculiar about him,—some originality and self-inspiration in his character, but none, or very little, in his intellect. Nevertheless, the lad himself seems to feel as if he were a genius. I like him well enough, however; but, after all, these originals in a small way, after one has seen a few of them, become more dull and commonplace than even those who keep the ordinary pathway of life. They have a rule and a routine, which they follow with as little variety as other people do their rule and routine; and when once we have fathomed their mystery, nothing can be more wearisome. An innate perception and reflection of truth give the only sort of originality that does not finally grow intolerable.

September 4th.—I made a voyage in the "Pond-Lily" all by myself yesterday morning, and was much encouraged by my success in causing the boat to go whither I would. I have always liked to be afloat, but I think I have never adequately conceived of the enjoyment till now, when I begin to feel a power over that which supports me. I suppose I must have felt something like this sense of triumph when I first learnt to swim; but I have forgotten it. Oh that I could run wild!—that is, that I could put myself into a true relation with Nature, and be on friendly terms with all congenial elements.

We had a thunder-storm last evening; and to-day has been a cool, breezy, autumnal day, such as my soul and body love.

September 18*th*.—How the summer time flits away, even while it seems to be loitering onward, arm in arm with autumn! Of late I have walked but little over the hills and through the woods, my leisure being chiefly occupied with my boat, which I have now learned to manage with tolerable skill. Yesterday afternoon I made a voyage alone up the North Branch of Concord river. There was a strong west wind blowing dead against me, which, together with the current, increased by the height of the water, made the first part of the passage pretty toilsome. The black river was all dimpled over with little eddies and whirlpools; and the breeze, moreover, caused the billows to beat against the bow of the boat, with a sound like the flapping of a bird's wing. The waterweeds, where they were discernible through the tawny water, were straight outstretched by the force of the current, looking as if they were forced to hold on to their roots with all their might. If for a moment I desisted from paddling, the head of the boat was swept round by the combined might of wind and tide. However, I toiled onward stoutly, and, entering the North Branch, soon found myself floating quietly along a tranquil stream, sheltered from the breeze by the woods and a lofty hill. The current, likewise, lingered along so gently that it was merely a pleasure to propel the boat against it. I never could have conceived that there was so beautiful a river-scene in Concord as this of the North Branch. The stream flows through the midmost privacy and deepest heart of a wood, which, as if but half satisfied with its presence, calm, gentle, and unobtrusive as it is, seems to crowd upon it, and barely to allow it passage; for the trees are rooted on the very verge of the water, and dip their pendent branches into it. On one side there is a high bank, forming the side of a hill, the Indian name of which I have forgotten, though Mr. Thoreau told it to me; and here, in some instances, the trees stand leaning over the river, stretching out their arms as if about to plunge in headlong. On the other side, the bank is almost on a level with the water; and there the quiet congregation of trees stood with feet in the flood, and fringed with foliage down to its very surface. Vines here and there twine themselves about bushes, or aspens, or alder-trees, and hang their clusters (though scanty and infrequent this season) so that I can reach them from my boat. I scarcely remember a scene of more complete and lovely seclusion than the passage of the river through this wood. Even an Indian canoe, in olden times, could not have floated onward in deeper solitude than my boat. I have never elsewhere had such an opportunity to observe how much more beautiful reflection is than what we call reality. The sky, and the clustering foliage on either hand, and the effect of sunlight as it found its way through the shade, giving lightsome hues in contrast with the quiet depth of the prevailing tints,—all these seemed unsurpassably beautiful when beheld in upper air. But on gazing downward, there they were, the same even to the minutest particular, yet arrayed in ideal beauty, which satisfied the spirit incomparably more than the actual scene. I am half convinced that the reflection is indeed the reality, the real thing which Nature imperfectly images to our grosser sense. At any rate, the disembodied shadow is nearest to the soul.

There were many tokens of autumn in this beautiful picture. Two or three of the trees were actually dressed in their coats of many colours,—the real scarlet and gold which they wear before they put on mourning. These stood on low, marshy spots, where a frost has probably touched them already. Others were of a light, fresh green, resembling the hues of spring, though this, likewise, is a token of decay. The great mass of the foliage, however, appears unchanged; but ever and anon down came a yellow leaf, half flitting upon the air, half falling through it, and finally settling upon the water. A multitude of these were floating here and there along the river, many of them curling upward, so as to form little boats, fit for fairies to voyage in. They looked strangely pretty, with yet a melancholy prettiness, as they floated along. The general aspect of the river, however, differed but little from that of summer,—at least the difference defies expression. It is more in the character of the rich yellow sunlight than in aught else. The water of the stream has now a thrill of autumnal coolness; yet whenever a broad gleam fell across it, through an interstice of the foliage, multitudes of insects were darting to and fro upon its surface. The sunshine, thus falling across the dark river, has a most beautiful effect. It burnishes it, as it were, and yet leaves it as dark as ever.

On my return, I suffered the boat to float almost of its own will down the stream, and caught fish enough for this morning's breakfast. But, partly from a qualm of conscience, I finally put them all into the water again, and saw them swim away as if nothing had happened.

Monday, October 10*th*.—A long while, indeed, since my last date. But the weather has been generally sunny and pleasant, though often very cold; and I cannot endure to waste anything so precious as autumnal sunshine by staying in the house. So I have spent almost all the daylight hours in the open air. My chief amusement has been boating up and down the river. A week or two ago (September 27 and 28) I went on a pedestrian excursion with Mr. Emerson, and was gone two days and one night, it being the first and only night that I have spent away from home. We were that night at the village of Harvard, and the next morning walked three miles farther, to the Shaker village, where we breakfasted. Mr. Emerson had a theological discussion with two of the Shaker brethren; but the particulars of it have faded from my memory; and all the other adventures of the tour have now so lost their freshness that I cannot adequately recall them. Wherefore, let them rest untold. I recollect nothing so well as the aspect of some fringed gentians, which we saw growing by the roadside, and which were so beautiful that I longed to turn back and pluck them. After an arduous journey, we arrived safe home in the afternoon of the second day,—the first time that I ever came home in my life; for I never had a home before. On Saturday of the same week, my friend D. R—— came to see us, and stayed till Tuesday morning. On Wednesday there was a cattle-show in the village, of which I would give a description, if it had possessed any picturesque points. The foregoing are the chief outward events of our life.

In the meantime autumn has been advancing, and is said to be a month earlier than usual. We had frosts, sufficient to kill the bean and squash-vines, more than a fortnight ago; but there has since been some of the most delicious Indian-summer weather that I ever experienced,—mild, sweet, perfect days, in which the warm sunshine seemed to embrace the earth and all earth's children with love and tenderness. Generally, however, the bright days have been vexed with winds from the north-west, somewhat too keen and high for comfort. These winds have strewn our avenue with withered leaves, although the trees still retain some density of foliage, which is now imbrowned or otherwise variegated by autumn. Our apples, too, have been falling, falling, falling; and we have picked the fairest of them from the dewy grass, and put them in our store-room and elsewhere. On Thursday, John Flint began to gather those which remained on the trees; and I suppose they will amount to nearly twenty barrels, or perhaps more. As usual when I have anything to sell, apples are very low indeed in price, and will not fetch me more than a dollar a barrel. I have sold my share of the potato-field for twenty dollars and ten bushels of potatoes for my own use. This may suffice for the economical history of our recent life.

12 *o'clock*, M.—Just now I heard a sharp tapping at the window of my study, and looking up from my book (a volume of Rabelais), behold! the head of a little bird, who seemed to demand admittance! He was probably attempting to get a fly, which was on the pane of glass against which he rapped; and on my first motion the feathered visitor took wing. This incident had a curious effect on me. It impressed me as if the bird had been a spiritual visitant, so strange was it that this little wild thing should seem to ask our hospitality.

November 8th.—I am sorry that our journal has fallen so into neglect; but I see no chance of amendment. All my scribbling propensities will be far more than gratified in writing nonsense for the press; so that any gratuitous labour of the pen becomes peculiarly distasteful. Since the last date we have paid a visit of nine days to Boston and Salem, whence we returned a week ago yesterday. Thus we lost above a week of delicious autumnal weather, which should have been spent in the woods or upon the river. Ever since our return, however, until to-day, there has been a succession of genuine Indian-summer days, with gentle winds or none at all, and a misty atmosphere, which idealizes all nature, and a mild, beneficent sunshine, inviting one to lie down in a nook and forget all earthly care. To-day the sky is dark and lowering, and occasionally lets fall a few sullen tears. I suppose we must bid farewell to Indian summer now, and expect no more love and tenderness from Mother Nature till next spring be well advanced. She has already made herself as unlovely in outward aspect as can well be. We took a walk to Sleepy Hollow yesterday, and beheld scarcely a green thing, except the everlasting verdure of the family of pines, which, indeed, are trees to thank God for at this season. A range of young birches had retained a pretty liberal colouring of yellow or tawny leaves, which became very cheerful in the sunshine. There were one or two oak-trees whose foliage still retained a deep, dusky red, which looked rich and warm; but most of the oaks had reached the last stage of autumnal decay,— the dusky brown hue. Millions of their leaves strew the woods, and rustle underneath the foot; but enough remain upon the boughs to make a melancholy harping when the wind sweeps over them. We found some fringed gentians in the meadow, most of them blighted and withered : but a few were quite perfect, The other day, since our return from Salem, I found a violet ; yet it was so cold that day, that a large pool of water, under the shadow of some trees, had remained frozen from morning till afternoon. The ice was so thick as not to be broken by some sticks and small stones which I threw upon it. But ice and snow too will soon be no extraordinary matters with us.

During the last week we have had three stoves put up, and henceforth no light of a cheerful fire will gladden us at eventide. Stoves are detestable in every respect, except that they keep us perfectly comfortable.

Thursday, November 24th.—This is Thanksgiving Day, a good old festival, and we have kept it with our hearts, and, besides, have made good cheer upon our turkey and pudding, and pies and custards, although none sat at our board but our two selves. There was a new and livelier sense, I think, that we have at last found a home, and that a new family has been gathered since the last Thanksgiving Day. There have been many bright, cold days latterly,— so cold that it has required a pretty rapid pace to keep one's self warm a-walking. Day before yesterday I saw a party of boys skating on a pond of water that has overflowed a neighbouring meadow. Running water has not yet frozen. Vegetation has quite come to a stand, except in a few sheltered spots. In a deep ditch we found a tall plant of the freshest and healthiest green, which looked as if it must have grown within the last few weeks. We wander among the wood-paths, which are very pleasant in the sunshine of the afternoons, the trees looking rich and warm,—such of them, I mean, as have retained their russet leaves ; and where the leaves are strewn along the paths, or heaped plentifully in some hollow of the hills, the effect is not without a charm. To-day the morning rose with rain, which has since changed to snow and sleet ; and now the landscape is as dreary as can well be imagined,—white, with the brownness of the soil and withered grass everywhere peeping out. The swollen river, of a leaden hue, drags itself sullenly along; and this may be termed the first winter's day.

Friday, March 31*st*, 1843.—The first month of spring is already gone; and still the snow lies deep on hill and valley, and the river is still frozen from bank to bank, although a late rain has caused pools of water to stand on the surface of the ice, and the meadows are overflowed into broad lakes. Such a protracted winter has not been known for twenty years, at least. I have almost forgotten the woodpaths and shady places which I used to know so well last summer; and my views are so much confined to the interior of our mansion, that sometimes, looking out of the window, I am surprised to catch a glimpse of houses, at no great distance, which had quite passed out of my recollection. From present appearances, another month may scarcely suffice to wash away all the snow from the open country; and in the woods and hollows it may linger yet longer. The winter will not have been a day less than five months long; and it would not be unfair to call it seven. A great space, indeed, to miss the smile of Nature, in a single year of human life. Even out of the midst of happiness I have sometimes sighed and groaned; for

I love the sunshine, and the greenwoods, and the sparkling blue water; and it seems as if the picture of our inward bliss should be set in a beautiful frame of outward nature. .... As to the daily course of our life, I have written with pretty commendable diligence, averaging from two to four hours a day; and the result is seen in various magazines. I might have written more, if it had seemed worth while; but I was content to earn only so much gold as might suffice for our immediate wants, having prospect of official station and emolument which would do away with the necessity of writing for bread. Those prospects have not yet had their fulfilment; and we are well content to wait, because an office would inevitably remove us from our present happy home,—at least from an outward home; for there is an inner one that will accompany us wherever we go. Meantime, the magazine people do not pay their debts; so that we taste some of the inconveniences of poverty. It is an annoyance, not a trouble.

Every day, I trudge through snow and slosh to the village, look into the post-office, and spend an hour at the reading-room; and then return home, generally without having spoken a word to a human being. .... In the way of exercise I saw and split wood, and, physically, I never was in a better condition than now. This is chiefly owing, doubtless, to a satisfied heart, in aid of which comes the exercise above mentioned, and about a fair proportion of intellectual labour.

On the 9th of this month, we left home again on a visit to Boston and Salem. I alone went to Salem, where I resumed all my bachelor habits for nearly a fortnight, leading the same life in which ten years of my youth flitted away like a dream. But how much changed was I! At last I had caught hold of a reality which never could be taken from me. It was good thus to get apart from my happiness, for the sake of contemplating it. On the 21st, I returned to Boston, and went out to Cambridge to dine with Longfellow, whom I had not seen since his return from Europe. The next day we came back to our old house, which had been deserted all this time; for our servant had gone with us to Boston.

Friday, April 7th.—My wife has gone to Boston to see her sister M——, who is to be married in two or three weeks, and then immediately to visit Europe for six months. . . . I betook myself to sawing and splitting wood—there being an inward unquietness which demanded active exercise—and I sawed, I think, more briskly than ever before. When I re-entered the house, it was with somewhat of a desolate feeling; yet not without an intermingled pleasure, as being the more conscious that all separation was temporary, and scarcely real, even for the little time that it may last. After my solitary dinner, I lay down, with the *Dial* in my hand, and attempted to sleep; but sleep would not come. . . . So I arose, and began this record in the journal, almost at the commencement of which I was interrupted by a visit from Mr. Thoreau, who came to return a book, and to announce his purpose of going to reside at Staten Island, as private tutor in the family of Mr. Emerson's brother. We had some conversation upon this subject, and upon the spiritual advantages of change of place, and upon the *Dial*, and upon Mr. Alcott, and other kindred or concatenated subjects. I am glad, on Mr. Thoreau's own account, that he is going away, as he is out of health, and may be benefited by his removal; but, on my account, I should like to have him remain here, he being one of the few persons, I think, with whom to hold intercourse is like hearing the wind among the boughs of a forest-tree; and, with all this wild freedom, there is high and classic cultivation in him too. . . .

I had a purpose, if circumstances would permit, of

passing the whole term of my wife's absence without speaking a word to any human being; but now my Pythagorean vow has been broken, within three or four hours after her departure.

Saturday, April 8th.—After journalizing yesterday afternoon, I went out and sawed and split wood till tea-time, then studied German (translating "Lenore"), with an occasional glance at a beautiful sunset, which I could not enjoy sufficiently by myself to induce me to lay aside the book. After lamplight, finished "Lenore," and drowsed over Voltaire's "Candide," occasionally refreshing myself with a tune from Mr. Thoreau's musical box, which he had left in my keeping. The evening was but a dull one.

I retired soon after nine, and felt some apprehension that the old doctor's ghost would take this opportunity to visit me; but I rather think his former visitations have not been intended for me, and that I am not sufficiently spiritual for ghostly communication. At all events, I met with no disturbance of the kind, and slept soundly enough till six o'clock or thereabouts. The forenoon was spent with the pen in my hand, and sometimes I had the glimmering of an idea, and endeavoured to materialize it in words; but on the whole my mind was idly vagrant, and refused to work to any systematic purpose. Between eleven and twelve I went to the post-office, but found no letter; then spent above an hour reading at the Athenæum. On my way home, I encountered Mr. Flint, for the first time these many weeks, although he is our next neighbour in one direction. I inquired if he could sell us some potatoes, and he promised to send half a bushel for trial. Also, he encouraged me to hope that he might buy a barrel of our apples. After my encounter with Mr. Flint, I returned to our lonely old abbey, opened the door without the usual heart-spring, ascended to my study, and began to read a tale of Tieck. Slow work, and dull work too! Anon, Molly, the cook, rang the bell for dinner,—a sumptuous banquet of stewed veal and macaroni, to which I sat down in solitary state. My appetite served me sufficiently to eat with, but not for enjoyment. Nothing has a zest in my present widowed state. [Thus far I had written, when Mr. Emerson called.] After dinner, I lay down on the couch, with the *Dial* in my hand as a soporific, and had a short nap; then began to journalize.

Mr. Emerson came, with a sunbeam in his face; and we had as good a talk as I ever remember to have had with him. He spoke of Margaret Fuller, who, he says, has risen perceptibly into a higher state since their last meeting. [There rings the tea-bell.] Then we discoursed of Ellery Channing, a volume of whose poems is to be immediately published, with revisions by Mr. Emerson himself and Mr. Sam G. Ward. .... He calls them "poetry for poets." Next Mr. Thoreau was discussed, and his approaching departure; in respect to which we agreed pretty well. .... We talked of Brook Farm, and the singular moral aspects which it presents, and the great desirability that its progress and developments should be observed and its history written; also of C. N———, who, it appears, is passing through a new moral phasis. He is silent, inexpressive, talks little or none, and listens without response, except a sardonic laugh; and some of his friends think that he is passing into permanent eclipse. Various other matters were considered or glanced at, and finally, between five and six o'clock, Mr. Emerson took his leave. I then went out to chop wood, my allotted space for which had been very much abridged by his visit; but I was not sorry. I went on with the journal for a few minutes before tea, and have finished the present record in the setting sunshine and gathering dusk. . .

Salem.—. . . . Here I am, in my old chamber, where I produced those stupendous works of fiction which have since impressed the universe with wonderment and awe! To this chamber, doubtless, in all succeeding ages, pilgrims will come to pay their tribute of reverence;—they will put off their shoes at the threshold for fear of desecrating the tattered old carpets! "There," they will exclaim, "is the very bed in which he slumbered, and where he was visited by those ethereal visions which he afterwards fixed for ever in glowing words! There is the wash stand at which this exalted personage cleansed himself from the stains of earth, and rendered his outward man a fitting exponent of the pure soul within! There, in its mahogany frame, is the dressing glass, which often reflected that noble brow, those hyacinthine locks, that mouth bright with smiles or tremulous with feeling, that flashing or melting eye, that—in short, every item of the magnanimous face of this unexampled man! There is the pine table,—there the old flag-bottomed chair on which he sat, and at which he scribbled, during his agonies of inspiration! There is the old chest of drawers in which he kept what shirts a poor author may be supposed to have possessed! There is the closet in which was reposited his threadbare suit of black! There is the worn-out shoe-brush with which this polished writer polished his boots! There is—" but I believe this will be pretty much all, so here I close the catalogue. . . . .

A cloudy veil stretches over the abyss of my nature. I have, however, no love of secrecy and darkness. I am glad to think that God sees through my heart, and, if any angel has power to penetrate into it, he is welcome to know everything that is there. Yes, and so may any mortal who is capable of full sympathy, and therefore worthy to come into my depths. But he must find his own way there. I can neither guide nor enlighten him. It is this involuntary reserve, I suppose, that has given the objectivity to my writings; and when people think that I am pouring myself out in a tale or an essay, I am merely telling what is common to human nature, not what is peculiar to myself. I sympathize with them, not they with me. . . . .

I have recently been both lectured about and preached about here in my native city; the preacher was Rev. Mr. Fox, of Newburyport; but how he contrived to put me into a sermon I know not. I trust he took for his text, "Behold an Israelite indeed, in whom there is no guile."

Salem, March 12th.—. . . . That poor home! how desolate it is now! Last night, being awake, ... my thoughts travelled back to the lonely old Manse; and it seemed as if I were wandering upstairs and downstairs all by myself. My fancy was almost afraid to be there alone. I could see every object in a dim grey light,—our chamber, the study, all in confusion; the parlour, with the fragments of that abortive breakfast on the table, and the precious silver forks, and the old bronze image, keeping its solitary stand upon the mantel-piece. Then, methought, the wretched Vigwiggie came, and jumped upon the window-sill, and clung there with her forepaws, mewing dismally for admittance, which I could not grant her, being there myself only in the spirit. And then came the ghost of the old doctor, stalking through the gallery, and down the staircase, and peeping into the parlour; and though I was wide awake, and conscious of being so many miles from the spot, still it was quite awful to think of the ghost having sole possession of our home; for I could not quite separate myself from it, after all. Somehow the Doctor and I seemed to be there *tête-à-tête.* . . . I believe I did not have any fantasies about the ghostly kitchen-maid; but I trust Mary left the flat-irons within her reach, so that she may do all her ironing while we are away, and never disturb us more at midnight. I suppose she comes thither to iron her shroud, and perhaps, likewise, to smooth the Doctor's band. Probably, during her lifetime, she allowed him to go to some ordination or other grand clerical celebration with rumpled linen; and ever since, and throughout all earthly futurity (at least, as long as the house shall stand), she is doomed to exercise a nightly toil with a spiritual flat-iron. Poor sinner!—and doubtless Satan heats the irons for her. What nonsense is all this! but, really, it does make me shiver to think of that poor home of ours.

March 16*th*.—. . . . As for this Mr.——, I wish he would not be so troublesome. His scheme is well enough, and might possibly become popular; but it has no peculiar advantages with reference to myself, nor do the subjects of his proposed books particularly suit my fancy as themes to write upon. Somebody else will answer his purpose just as well; and I would rather write books of my own imagining than be hired to develop the ideas of an engraver; especially as the pecuniary prospect is not better, nor so good, as it might be elsewhere. I intend to adhere to my former plan of writing one or two mythological story-books, to be published under O'Sullivan's auspices in New York,—which is the only place where books can be published with a chance of profit. As a matter of courtesy, I may call on Mr.——if I have time ; but I do not intend to be connected with this affair.

Sunday, April 9th.—. . . . After finishing my record in the journal, I sat a long time in grandmother's chair, thinking of many things. . . . . My spirits were at a lower ebb than they ever descend to when I am not alone ; nevertheless, neither was I absolutely sad. Many times I wound and rewound Mr. Thoreau's little musical box ; but certainly its peculiar sweetness had evaporated, and I am pretty sure that I should throw it out of the window were I doomed to hear it long and often. It has not an infinite soul. When it was almost as dark as the moonlight would let it be, I lighted the lamp, and went on with Tieck's tale, slowly and painfully, often wishing for help in my difficulties. At last I determined to learn a little about pronouns and verbs before proceeding further, and so took up the phrase-book, with which I was commendably busy, when, at about a quarter to nine, came a knock at my study-door, and, behold, there was Molly with a letter!

How she came by it I did not ask, being content to suppose it was brought by a heavenly messenger. I had not expected a letter; and what a comfort it was to me in my loneliness and sombreness! I called Molly to take her note (enclosed), which she received with a face of delight as broad and bright as the kitchen fire. Then I read, and re-read, and re-re-read, and quadruply, quintuply, and sextuply re-read my epistle, until I had it all by heart, and then continued to re-read it for the sake of the penmanship. Then I took up the phrase-book again; but could not study, and so bathed and retired, it being now not far from ten o'clock. I lay awake a good deal in the night, but saw no ghost.

I arose about seven, and found that the upper part of my nose, and the region round about, was grievously discoloured: and at the angle of the left eye there is a great spot of almost black purple, and a broad streak of the same hue semicircling beneath either eye, while green, yellow, and orange overspread the circumjacent country. It looks not unlike a gorgeous sunset, throwing its splendour over the heaven of my countenance. It will behove me to show myself as little as possible, else people will think I have fought a pitched battle. . . . . The

Devil take the stick of wood! What had I done, that it should bemaul me so? However, there is no pain, though, I think, a very slight affection of the eyes.

This forenoon I began to write, and caught an idea by the skirts, which I intend to hold fast, though it struggles to get free. As it was not ready to be put upon paper, however, I took up the *Dial*, and finished reading the article on Mr. Alcott. It is not very satisfactory, and it has not taught me much. Then I read Margaret's article on Canova, which is good. About this time the dinner-bell rang, and I went down without much alacrity, though with a good appetite enough. . . . . It was in the angle of my *right* eye, not my left, that the blackest purple was collected. But they both look like the very Devil.

Half-past five o'clock.—After writing the above,. . . . I again set to work on Tieck's tale, and worried through several pages; and then, at half-past four, threw open one of the western windows of my study, and sallied forth to take the sunshine. I went down through the orchard to the river-side. The orchard-path is still deeply covered with snow; and so is the whole visible universe, except streaks upon the hillsides, and spots in the sunny hollows, where the brown earth peeps through. The river, which a few days ago was entirely imprisoned, has now broken its fetters; but a tract of ice extended across from near the foot of the monument to the abutment of the old bridge, and looked so solid that I supposed it would yet remain for a day or two. Large cakes and masses of ice came floating down the current, which, though not very violent, hurried along at a much swifter pace than the ordinary one of our sluggish river-god. These ice-masses, when they struck the barrier of ice above mentioned, acted upon it like a battering-ram, and were themselves forced high out of the water, or sometimes carried beneath the main sheet of ice. At last, down the stream came an immense mass of ice, and, striking the barrier about at its centre, it gave way, and the whole was swept onward together, leaving the river entirely free, with only here and there a cake of ice floating quietly along. The great accumulation, in its downward course, hit against a tree that stood in mid-current, and caused it to quiver like a reed; and it swept quite over the shrubbery that bordered what, in summer-time, is the river's bank, but which is now nearly the centre of the stream. Our river in its present state has quite a noble breadth. The little hillock which formed the abutment of the old bridge is now an island with its tuft of trees. Along the hither shore a row of trees stand up to their knees, and the smaller ones to their middles, in the water; and afar off, on the surface of the stream, we see tufts of bushes emerging, thrusting up their heads, as it were, to breathe. The water comes over the stone wall, and encroaches several yards on the boundaries of our orchard. [Here the supper-bell rang.] If our boat were in good order, I should now set forth on voyages of discovery, and visit nooks on the borders of the meadows, which by and by will be a mile or two from the water's edge. But she is in very bad condition, full of water, and, doubtless, as leaky as a sieve.

On coming from supper, I found that little Puss had established herself in the study, probably with intent to pass the night here. She now lies on the footstool between my feet, purring most obstreperously. The day of my wife's departure, she came to me, talking with the greatest earnestness; but whether it was to condole with me on my loss, or to demand my redoubled care for herself, I could not well make out. As Puss now constitutes a third part of the family, this mention of her will not appear amiss. How Molly employs herself, I know not. Once in a while, I hear a door slam like a thunder-clap; but she never shows her face, nor speaks a word, unless to announce a visitor or deliver a letter. This day, on my part, will have been spent without exchanging a syllable with any human being, unless something unforeseen should yet call for the exercise of speech before bedtime.

Monday, April 10*th.*—I sat till eight o'clock, meditating upon this world and the next, ... and sometimes dimly shaping out scenes of a tale. Then betook myself to the German phrase-book. Ah! these are but dreary evenings. The lamp would not brighten my spirits, though it was duly filled. . . . This forenoon was spent in scribbling, by no means to my satisfaction, until past eleven, when I went to the village. Nothing in our box at the post-office. I read during the customary hour, or more, at the Athenæum, and returned without saying a word to mortal. I gathered, from some conversation that I heard, that a son of Adam is to be buried this afternoon from the meeting-house; but the name of the deceased escaped me. It is no great matter, so it be but written in the Book of Life.

My variegated face looks somewhat more human

to-day; though I was unaffectedly ashamed to meet anybody's gaze, and therefore turned my back or my shoulder as much as possible upon the world. At dinner, behold an immense joint of roast-veal! I would willingly have had some assistance in the discussion of this great piece of calf. I am ashamed to eat alone; it becomes the mere gratification of animal appetite,— the tribute which we are compelled to pay to our grosser nature; whereas in the company of another it is refined and moralized and spiritualized; and over our earthly victuals (or rather *vittles*, for the former is a very foolish mode of spelling),—over our earthly vittles is diffused a sauce of lofty and gentle thoughts, and tough meat is mollified with tender feelings. But oh! these solitary meals are the dismallest part of my present experience. When the company rose from table, they all, in my single person, ascended to the study, and employed themselves in reading the article on Oregon in the *Democratic Review*. Then they plodded onward in the rugged and bewildering depths of Tieck's tale until five o'clock, when, with one accord, they went out to split wood. This has been a grey day, with now and then a sprinkling of snow-flakes through the air. . . . To-day no more than yesterday have I spoken a word to mortal. . . . It is now sunset, and I must meditate till dark.

April 11*th.*—I meditated accordingly, but without any very wonderful result. Then at eight o'clock bothered myself till after nine with this eternal tale of Tieck. The forenoon was spent in scribbling; but at eleven o'clock my thoughts ceased to flow,—indeed, their current has been woefully interrupted all along, —so I threw down my pen, and set out on the daily journey to the village. Horrible walking! I wasted the customary hour at the Athenæum, and returned home, if home it may now be called. Till dinner-time I laboured on Tieck's tale, and resumed that agreeable employment after the banquet.

Just when I was on the point of choking with a huge German word, Molly announced Mr. Thoreau. He wished to take a row in the boat, for the last time, perhaps, before he leaves Concord. So we emptied the water out of her, and set forth on our voyage. She leaks, but not more than she did in the autumn. We rowed to the foot of the hill which borders the North Branch, and there landed, and climbed the moist and snowy hillside for the sake of the prospect. Looking down the river, it might well have been mistaken for an arm of the sea, so broad is now its swollen tide; and I could have fancied that, beyond one other headland, the mighty ocean would outspread itself before the eye. On our return we boarded a large cake of ice, which was floating down the river, and were borne by it directly to our own landing-place, with the boat towing behind.

Parting with Mr. Thoreau, I spent half an hour in chopping wood, when Molly informed me that Mr. Emerson wished to see me. He had brought a letter of Ellery Channing, written in a style of very pleasant humour. This being read and discussed, together with a few other matters, he took his leave, since which I have been attending to my journalizing duty; and thus this record is brought down to the present moment.

April 25*th.*—Spring is advancing, sometimes with sunny days, and sometimes, as is the case now, with chill, moist, sullen ones. There is an influence in the season that makes it almost impossible for me to bring my mind down to literary employment; perhaps because several months' pretty constant work has exhausted that species of energy,—perhaps because in spring it is more natural to labour actively than to think. But my impulse now is to be idle altogether,—to lie in the sun, or wander about and look at the revival of Nature from her deathlike slumber, or to be borne down the current of the river in my boat. If I had wings, I would gladly fly; yet would prefer to be wafted along by a breeze, sometimes alighting on a patch of green grass, then gently whirled away to a still sunnier spot. . . . Oh, how blest should I be were there nothing to do! Then I would watch every inch and hair's breadth of the progress of the season; and not a leaf should put itself forth, in the vicinity of our old mansion, without my noting it. But now, with the burden of a continual task upon me, I have not freedom of mind to make such observations. I merely see what is going on in a very general way. The snow, which, two or three weeks ago, covered hill and valley, is now diminished to one or two solitary specks in the visible landscape; though doubtless there are still heaps of it in the shady places in the woods. There have been no violent rains to carry it off: it has diminished gradually, inch by inch, and day after day; and I observed, along the roadside, that the green blades of grass had sometimes sprouted on the very edge of the snow-drift the moment that the earth was uncovered.

The pastures and grass-fields have not yet a general effect of green; nor have they that cheerless brown tint which they wear in later autumn, when vegetation has entirely ceased. There is now a suspicion of verdure,—the faint shadow of it,—but not the warm reality. Sometimes, in a happy exposure, —there is one such tract across the river, the carefully cultivated mowing-field, in front of an old red homestead,—such patches of land wear a beautiful and tender green, which no other season will equal; because, let the grass be green as it may hereafter, it will not be so set off by surrounding barrenness. The trees in our orchard, and elsewhere, have as yet no leaves; yet to the most careless eye they appear full of life and vegetable blood. It seems as if, by one magic touch, they might instantaneously put forth all their foliage, and the wind, which now sighs through their naked branches, might all at once find itself impeded by innumerable leaves. This sudden development would be scarcely more wonderful than the gleam of verdure which often brightens, in a moment, as it were, along the slope of a bank or roadside. It is like a gleam of sunlight. Just now it was brown, like the rest of the scenery: look again, and there is an apparition of green grass. The Spring, no doubt, comes onward with fleeter footsteps, because Winter has lingered so long that, at best, she can hardly retrieve half the allotted term of her reign.

The river, this season, has encroached farther on the land than it has been known to do for twenty years past. It has formed along its course a succession of lakes, with a current through the midst. My boat has lain at the bottom of the orchard, in very convenient proximity to the house. It has borne me over stone fences; and, a few days ago, Ellery Channing and I passed through two rails into the great northern road, along which we paddled for some distance. The trees have a singular appearance in the midst of waters. The curtailment of their trunks quite destroys the proportions of the whole tree; and we become conscious of a regularity and propriety in the forms of Nature, by the effect of this abbreviation. The waters are now subsiding, but gradually. Islands become annexed to the mainland, and other islands emerge from the flood, and will soon, likewise, be connected with the continent. We have seen on a small scale the process of the deluge, and can now witness that of the reappearance of the earth.

Crows visited us long before the snow was off. They seem mostly to have departed now, or else to have betaken themselves to remote depths of the woods, which they haunt all summer long. Ducks came in great numbers, and many sportsmen went in pursuit of them, along the river, but they also have disappeared. Gulls come up from seaward, and soar high overhead, flapping their broad wings in the upper sunshine. They are among the most picturesque birds that I am acquainted with; indeed, quite the most so, because the manner of their flight makes them almost stationary parts of the landscape. The imagination has time to rest upon them; they have not flitted away in a moment. You go up among the clouds, and lay hold of these soaring gulls, and repose with them upon the sustaining atmosphere. The smaller birds,—the birds that build their nests in our trees, and sing for us at morning-red, I will not describe. . . . But I must mention the great companies of blackbirds—more than the famous "four-and-twenty" who were baked in a pie—that congregate on the tops of contiguous trees, and vociferate with all the clamour of a turbulent political meeting. Politics must certainly be the subject of such a tumultuous debate; but still there is a melody in each individual utterance, and a harmony in the general effect. Mr. Thoreau tells me that these noisy assemblages consist of three different species of blackbirds ; but I forget the other two. Robins have been long among us, and swallows have more recently arrived.

April 26th.—Here is another misty day, muffling the sun. The lilac shrubs under my study-window are almost in leaf. In two or three days more I may put forth my hand and pluck a green bough. These lilacs appear to be very aged, and have lost the luxuriant foliage of their prime. Old age has a singular aspect in lilacs, rose-bushes, and other ornamental shrubs. It seems as if such things, as they grow only for beauty, ought to flourish in immortal youth, or at least to die before their decrepitude. They are trees of Paradise, and therefore not naturally subject to decay ; but have lost their birthright by being transplanted hither. There is a kind of ludicrous unfitness in the idea of a venerable rose-bush ; and there is something analogous to this in human life. Persons who can only be graceful and ornamental—who can give the world nothing but flowers—should die young, and never be seen with grey hairs and wrinkles, any more than the flower-shrubs with mossy bark and scanty foliage, like the lilacs under my window. Not that beauty is not worthy of immortality. Nothing else, indeed, is worthy of it; and thence, perhaps, the sense of impropriety when we see it triumphed over by time. Apple-trees, on the other hand, grow old without reproach. Let them live as long as they may, and contort themselves in whatever fashion they please, they are still respectable, even if they afford us only an apple or two in a season, or none at all. Human flower-shrubs, if they will grow old on earth, should, beside their lovely blossoms, bear some kind of fruit that will satisfy earthly appetites; else men will not be satisfied that the moss should gather on them.

Winter and spring are now struggling for the mastery in my study; and I yield somewhat to each, and wholly to neither. The window is open, and there is a fire in the stove. The day when the window is first thrown open should be an epoch in the year; but I have forgotten to record it. Seventy or eighty springs have visited this old house; and sixty of them found old Dr. Ripley here,—not always old, it is true, but gradually getting wrinkles and grey hairs, and looking more and more the picture of winter. But he was no flower-shrub, but one of those fruit-trees or timber-trees that acquire a grace with their old age.

Last spring found this house solitary for the first time since it was built; and now again she peeps into our open windows and finds new faces here.

It is remarkable how much uncleanness winter brings with it, or leaves behind it. . . . . The yard, garden, and avenue, which should be my department, require a great amount of labour. The avenue is strewed with withered leaves, — the whole crop, apparently, of last year,—some of which are now raked into heaps; and we intend to make a bonfire of them. . . . . There are quantities of decayed branches, which one tempest after another has flung down, black and rotten. In the garden are the old cabbages which we did not think worth gathering last autumn, and the dry bean-vines, and the withered stalks of the asparagus-bed; in short, all the wrecks of the departed year,—its mouldering relics, its dry bones. It is a pity that the world cannot be made over anew every spring. Then, in the yard, there are the piles of firewood, which I ought to have sawed and thrown into the shed long since, but which will cumber the earth, I fear, till June, at least. Quantities of chips are strewn about, and on removing them we find the yellow stalks of grass sprouting underneath. Nature does her best to beautify this disarray. The grass springs up most industriously, especially in sheltered and sunny angles of the buildings, or round the doorsteps,—a locality which seems particularly favourable to its growth; for it is already high enough to bend over and wave in the wind. I was surprised to observe that some weeds (especially a plant that stains the fingers with its yellow juice) had lived, and retained their freshness and sap as perfectly as in summer, through all the frosts and snows of last winter. I saw them, the last green thing, in the autumn; and here they are again, the first in the spring.

Thursday, April 27th.—I took a walk into the fields, and round our opposite hill, yesterday noon, but made no very remarkable observation. The frogs have begun their concerts, though not as yet with a full choir. I found no violets nor anemones, nor anything in the likeness of a flower, though I looked carefully along the shelter of the stone walls, and in all spots apparently propitious. I ascended the hill, and had a wide prospect of a swollen river, extending around me in a semi-circle of three or four miles, and rendering the view much finer than in summer, had there only been foliage. It seemed like the formation of a new world; for islands were everywhere emerging, and capes extending forth into the flood; and these tracts, which were thus won from the watery empire, were among the greenest in the landscape. The moment the deluge leaves them, Nature asserts them to be her property by covering them with verdure; or perhaps the grass had been growing under the water. On the hill-top where I stood, the grass had scarcely begun to sprout; and I observed that even those places which looked greenest in the distance were but scantily grass-covered when I actually reached them. It was hope that painted them so bright.

Last evening we saw a bright light on the river, betokening that a boat's party were engaged in spearing fish. It looked like a descended star,—like red Mars,—and, as the water was perfectly smooth, its gleam was reflected downward into the depths. It is a very picturesque sight. In the deep quiet of the night I suddenly heard the light and lively note of a bird from a neighbouring tree,—a real song, such as those which greet the purple dawn, or mingle with the yellow sunshine. What could the little bird mean by pouring it forth at midnight? Probably the note gushed out from the midst of a dream, in which he fancied himself in Paradise with his mate;

and, suddenly awaking, he found he was on a cold, leafless bough, with a New England mist penetrating through his feathers. That was a sad exchange of imagination for reality; but if he found his mate beside him, all was well.

This is another misty morning, ungenial in aspect, but kinder than it looks; for it paints the hills and valleys with a richer brush than the sunshine could. There is more verdure now than when I looked out of the window an hour ago. The willow-tree opposite my study window is ready to put forth its leaves. There are some objections to willows. It is not a dry and cleanly tree; it impresses me with an association of sliminess; and no trees, I think, are perfectly satisfactory, which have not a firm and hard texture of trunk and branches. But the willow is almost the earliest to put forth its leaves, and the last to scatter them on the ground; and during the whole winter its yellow twigs give it a sunny aspect, which is not without a cheering influence in a proper point of view. Our old house would lose much were this willow to be cut down, with its golden crown over the roof in winter, and its heap of summer verdure. The present Mr. Ripley planted it, fifty years ago, or thereabouts.

Friday, June 2nd.—Last night there came a frost, which has done great damage to my garden. The beans have suffered very much, although, luckily, not more than half that I planted have come up. The squashes, both summer and winter, appear to be almost killed. As to the other vegetables, there is little mischief done,—the potatoes not being yet above ground, except two or three; and the peas and corn are of a hardier nature. It is sad that Nature will so sport with us poor mortals, inviting us with sunny smiles to confide in her; and then, when we are entirely in her power, striking us to the heart. Our summer commences at the latter end of June, and terminates somewhere about the first of August. There are certainly not more than six weeks of the whole year when a frost may be deemed anything remarkable.

Friday, June 23rd.—Summer has come at last,— the longest days, with blazing sunshine, and fervid heat. Yesterday glowed like molten brass. Last night was the most uncomfortably and unsleepably sultry that we have experienced since our residence in Concord; and to-day it scorches again. I have a sort of enjoyment in these seven times heated furnaces of midsummer, even though they make me droop like a thirsty plant. The sunshine can scarcely be too burning for my taste; but I am no enemy to summer showers. Could I only have the freedom to be perfectly idle now,—no duty to fulfil, no mental or physical labour to perform,— I should be as happy as a squash, and much in the same mode; but the necessity of keeping my brain at work eats into my comfort, as the squash-bugs do into the heart of the vines. I keep myself uneasy and produce little, and almost nothing that is worth producing.

The garden looks well now: the potatoes flourish; the early corn waves in the wind; the squashes, both for summer and winter use, are more forward, I suspect, than those of any of my neighbours. I am forced, however, to carry on a continual warfare with the squash-bugs, who, were I to let them alone for a day, would perhaps quite destroy the prospects of the whole summer. It is impossible not to feel angry with these unconscionable insects, who scruple not to do such excessive mischief to me, with only the profit of a meal or two to themselves. For their own sakes they ought at least to wait till the squashes are better grown. Why is it, I wonder, that Nature has provided such a host of enemies for every useful esculent, while the weeds are suffered to grow unmolested, and are provided with such tenacity of life, and such methods of propagation, that the gardener must maintain a continual struggle or they will hopelessly overwhelm him? What hidden virtue is in these things, that it is granted them to sow themselves with the wind, and to grapple the earth with this immitigable stubbornness, and to flourish in spite of obstacles, and never to suffer blight beneath any sun or shade, but always to mock their enemies with the same wicked luxuriance? It is truly a mystery, and also a symbol. There is a sort of sacredness about them. Perhaps, if we could penetrate Nature's secrets, we should find that what we call weeds are more essential to the well-being of the world than the most precious fruit or grain. This may be doubted, however, for there is an unmistakable analogy between these wicked weeds and the bad habits and sinful propensities which have overrun the moral world; and we may as well imagine that there is good in one as in the other.

Our pease are in such forwardness that I should not wonder if we had some of them on the table within a week. The beans have come up ill, and I planted a fresh supply only the day before yesterday. We have watermelons in good advancement, and muskmelons also within three or four days. I set out some tomatoes last night, also some capers. It is my purpose to plant some more corn at the end of the month, or sooner. There ought to be a record of the flower-garden, and of the procession of the wild-flowers, as minute, at least, as of the kitchen vegetables and pot-herbs. Above all, the noting of the appearance of the first roses should not be omitted; nor of the Arethusa, one of the delicatest, gracefullest, and in every manner sweetest of the whole race of flowers. For a fortnight past I have found it in the swampy meadows, growing up to its chin in heaps of wet moss. Its hue is a delicate pink, of various depths of shade, and somewhat in the form of a Grecian helmet. To describe it is a feat beyond my power. Also the visit of two friends, who may fitly enough be mentioned among flowers, ought to have been described. Mrs. F. S—— and Miss A. S——. Also I have neglected to mention the birth of a little white dove.

I never observed, until the present season, how long and late the twilight lingers in these longest days. The orange hue of the western horizon remains till ten o'clock, at least, and how much later I am unable to say. The night before last, I could distinguish letters by this lingering gleam between nine and ten o'clock. The dawn, I suppose, shows itself as early as two o'clock, so that the absolute dominion of night has dwindled to almost nothing. There seems to be also a diminished necessity, or, at all events, a much less possibility, of sleep than at other periods of the year. I get scarcely any sound repose just now. It is summer, and not winter, that steals away mortal life. Well, we get the value of what is taken from us.

Saturday, July 1st.—We had our first dish of green pease (a very small one) yesterday. Every day for the last week has been tremendously hot; and our garden flourishes like Eden itself, only Adam could hardly have been doomed to contend with such a ferocious banditti of weeds.

Sunday, July 9th.—I know not what to say, and yet cannot be satisfied without marking with a word or two this anniversary. . . . . But life now swells and heaves beneath me like a brim-full ocean; and the endeavour to comprise any portion of it in words

is like trying to dip up the ocean in a goblet. . . . .
God bless and keep us! for there is something more
awful in happiness than in sorrow,—the latter being
earthly and finite, the former composed of the substance and texture of eternity, so that spirits still
embodied may well tremble at it.

July 18*th*.—This morning I gathered our first
summer-squashes. We should have had them some
days earlier, but for the loss of two of the vines, either
by a disease of the roots or by those infernal bugs.
We have had turnips and carrots several times.
Currants are now ripe, and we are in the full enjoyment
of cherries, which turn out much more delectable than
I anticipated. George Hillard and Mrs. Hillard paid
us a visit on Saturday last. On Monday afternoon he
left us, and Mrs. Hillard still remains here.

Friday, *July* 28*th*.—We had green corn for dinner
yesterday, and shall have some more to day, not quite
full-grown, but sufficiently so to be palatable. There
has been no rain, except one moderate shower, for
many weeks; and the earth appears to be wasting
away in a slow fever. This weather, I think, affects
the spirits very unfavourably. There is an irksome-

ness, a restlessness, a pervading dissatisfaction, together with an absolute incapacity to bend the mind to any serious effort. With me, as regards literary production, the summer has been unprofitable; and I only hope that my forces are recruiting themselves for the autumn and winter. For the future, I shall endeavour to be so diligent nine months of the year that I may allow myself a full and free vacation of the other three.

Monday, July 31st.—We had our first cucumber yesterday. There were symptoms of rain on Saturday, and the weather has since been as moist as the thirstiest soul could desire.

Wednesday, September 13th.—There was a frost the night before last, according to George Prescott; but no effects of it were visible in our garden. Last night, however, there was another, which has nipped the leaves of the winter-squashes and cucumbers, but seems to have done no other damage. This is a beautiful morning, and promises to be one of those heavenly days that render autumn, after all, the most delightful season of the year. We mean to make a voyage on the river this afternoon.

Sunday, September 23rd.—I have gathered the two last of our summer-squashes to-day. They have lasted ever since the 18th of July, and have numbered fifty-eight edible ones, of excellent quality. Last Wednesday, I think, I harvested our winter squashes, sixty-three in number, and mostly of fine size. Our last series of green corn, planted about the 1st of July, was good for eating two or three days ago. We still have beans; and our tomatoes, though backward, supply us with a dish every day or two. My potato-crop promises well; and, on the whole, my first independent experiment of agriculture is quite a successful one.

This is a glorious day,—bright, very warm, yet with an unspeakable gentleness both in its warmth and brightness. On such days it is impossible not to love Nature, for she evidently loves us. At other seasons she does not give me this impression, or only at very rare intervals; but in these happy, autumnal days, when she has perfected the harvests, and accomplished every necessary thing that she had to do, she overflows with a blessed superfluity of love. It is good to be alive now. Thank God for breath,—yes, for mere breath! when it is made up of such a heavenly breeze as this. It comes to the cheek with a real kiss; it would linger fondly around us, if it might; but, since it must be gone, it caresses us with its whole kindly heart, and passes onward, to caress likewise the next thing that it meets. There is a pervading blessing diffused over all the world. I look out of the window and think, "O perfect day! O beautiful world! O good God!" And such a day is the promise of a blissful eternity. Our Creator would never have made such weather, and given us the deep heart to enjoy it, above and beyond all thought, if He had not meant us to be immortal. It opens the gates of heaven, and gives us glimpses far inward.

Bless me! this flight has carried me a great way; so now let me come back to our old abbey. Our orchard is fast ripening; and the apples and great thumping pears strew the grass in such abundance that it becomes almost a trouble—though a pleasant one—to gather them. This happy breeze, too, shakes them down, as if it flung fruit to us out of the sky; and often, when the air is perfectly still, I hear the quiet fall of a great apple. Well, we are rich in blessings, though poor in money. . . .

Friday, October 6th.—Yesterday afternoon I took a solitary walk to Walden Pond. It was a cool, windy day, with heavy clouds rolling and tumbling about the sky, but still a prevalence of genial autumn sunshine. The fields are still green, and the great masses of the woods have not yet assumed their many-coloured garments; but here and there are solitary oaks of deep, substantial red, or maples of a more brilliant hue, or chestnuts either yellow or of a tenderer green than in summer. Some trees seem to return to their hue of May or early June before they put on the brighter autumnal tints. In some places, along the borders of low and moist land, a whole range of trees were clothed in the perfect gorgeousness of autumn, of all shades of brilliant colour, looking like the palette on which Nature was arranging the tints wherewith to paint a picture. These hues appeared to be thrown together without design; and yet there was perfect harmony among them, and a softness and a delicacy made up of a thousand different brightnesses. There is not, I think, so much contrast among these colours as might at first appear. The more you consider them, the more they seem to have one element among them all, which is the reason that the most brilliant display of them soothes the observer, instead of exciting him. And I know not whether it be more a moral effect or a physical one, operating merely on the eye; but it is a pensive gaiety, which causes a sigh often, and never a smile. We never fancy, for instance, that these gaily-clad trees might be changed into young damsels in holiday attire, and betake themselves to dancing on the plain. If they were to undergo such a transformation, they would surely arrange themselves in funeral procession, and go sadly along, with their purple and scarlet and golden garments trailing over the withering grass. When the sunshine falls upon them, they seem to smile; but it is as if they were heart-broken. But it is in vain for me to attempt to describe these autumnal brilliancies, or to convey the impression which they make on me. I have tried a thousand times, and always without the slightest self-satisfaction. Fortunately there is no need of such a record, for Nature renews the picture year after year; and even when we shall have passed away from the world, we can spiritually create these scenes, so that we may dispense with all efforts to put them into words.

Walden Pond was clear and beautiful as usual. It tempted me to bathe; and though the water was thrillingly cold, it was like the thrill of a happy death. Never was there such transparent water as this. I threw sticks into it, and saw them float suspended on an almost invisible medium. It seemed as if the pure air were beneath them, as well as above. It is fit for baptisms; but one would not wish it to be polluted by having sins washed into it. None but angels should bathe in it; but blessed babies might be dipped into its bosom.

In a small and secluded dell that opens upon the most beautiful cove of the whole lake, there is a little hamlet of huts or shanties, inhabited by the Irish people who are at work upon the railroad. There are three or four of these habitations, the very rudest, I should imagine, that civilized men ever made for themselves,—constructed of rough boards, with the protruding ends. Against some of them the earth is heaped up to the roof, or nearly so; and when the grass has had time to sprout upon them, they will look like small natural hillocks, or a species of ant-hills,—something in which Nature has a larger share than man. These huts are placed beneath the trees, oaks, walnuts, and white pines, wherever the trunks give them space to stand; and by thus adapting themselves to natural interstices, instead of making new ones, they do not break or disturb the solitude and seclusion of the place. Voices are heard, and the shouts and laughter of children, who play about like the sunbeams that come down through the branches.

Women are washing in open spaces, and long lines of whitened clothes are extended from tree to tree, fluttering and gambolling in the breeze. A pig, in a sty even more extemporary than the shanties, is grunting and poking his snout through the clefts of his habitation. The household pots and kettles are seen at the doors, and a glance within shows the rough benches that serve for chairs, and the bed upon the floor. The visitor's nose takes note of the fragrance of a pipe. And yet, with all these homely items, the repose and sanctity of the old wood do not seem to be destroyed or profaned. It overshadows these poor people, and assimilates them somehow or other to the character of its natural inhabitants. Their presence did not shock me any more than if I had merely discovered a squirrel's nest in a tree. To be sure, it is a torment to see the great, high, ugly embankment of the railroad, which is here thrusting itself into the lake, or along its margin, in close vicinity to this picturesque little hamlet. I have seldom seen anything more beautiful than the cove on the border of which the huts are situated; and the more I looked the lovelier it grew. The trees overshadowed it deeply; but on one side there was some brilliant shrubbery, which seemed to light up the whole picture with the effect of a sweet and melancholy smile. I felt as if spirits were there,—or as if these shrubs had a spiritual life. In short, the impression was indefinable; and, after gazing and musing a good while, I retraced my steps through the Irish hamlet, and plodded on along a wood-path.

According to my invariable custom, I mistook my way, and emerging upon the road, I turned my back instead of my face towards Concord, and walked on very diligently till a guide-board informed me of my mistake. I then turned about, and was shortly overtaken by an old yeoman in a chaise, who kindly offered me a drive, and soon set me down in the village.

[EXTRACTS FROM LETTERS.]

May 27th, 1844.— . . . My cook fills his office admirably. He prepared what I must acknowledge to be the best dish of fried fish and potatoes for dinner to-day that I ever tasted in this house. I scarcely recognized the fish of our own river. I make him get all the dinners, while I confine myself to the much lighter task of breakfast and tea. He also takes his turn in washing the dishes.

We had a very pleasant dinner at Longfellow's,

and I liked Mrs. Longfellow very much. The dinner was late and we sat long ; so that C—— and I did not get to Concord till half-past nine o'clock, and truly the old Manse seemed somewhat dark and desolate. The next morning George Prescott came with Una's Lion, who greeted me very affectionately, but whined and moaned as if he missed somebody who should have been here. I am not quite so strict as I should be in keeping him out of the house ; but I commiserate him and myself, for are we not both of us bereaved ? C——, whom I can no more keep from smoking than I could the kitchen chimney, has just come into the study with a cigar, which might perfume this letter and make you think it came from my own enormity, so I may as well stop here.

May 29th.—C—— is leaving me, to my unspeakable relief ; for he has had a bad cold, which caused him to be much more troublesome and less amusing than might otherwise have been the case.

May 31st.— . . . I get along admirably, and am at this moment superintending the corned beef, which has been on the fire, as it appears to me, ever since the beginning of time, and shows no symptom of being done before the crack of doom. Mrs. Hale says it must boil till it becomes tender; and so it shall, if I can find wood to keep the fire a-going.

Meantime, I keep my station in the dining-room, and read or write as composedly as in my own study. Just now, there came a very important rap at the front door, and I threw down a smoked herring which I had begun to eat, as there is no hope of the corned beef to-day, and went to admit the visitor. Who should it be but Ben B——, with a very peculiar and mysterious grin upon his face. He put into my hand a missive directed to "Mr. and Mrs. Hawthorne." It contained a little bit of card, signifying that Dr. L. F—— and Miss C. B—— receive their friends Thursday eve, June 6. I am afraid I shall be too busy washing my dishes to pay many visits. The washing of dishes does seem to me the most absurd and unsatisfactory business that I ever undertook. If, when once washed, they would remain clean for ever and ever (which they ought in all reason to do, considering how much trouble it is), there would be less occasion to grumble; but no sooner is it done, than it requires to be done again. On the whole, I have come to the resolution not to use more than one dish at each meal. However, I moralize deeply on this and other matters, and have discovered that all the trouble and affliction in the world come from the necessity of cleansing away our earthly stains.

I ate the last morsel of bread yesterday, and congratulate myself on being now reduced to the fag-end of necessity. Nothing worse can happen, according to ordinary modes of thinking, than to want bread; but, like most afflictions, it is more in prospect than reality. I found one cracker in the tureen, and exulted over it as if it had been so much gold. However, I have sent a petition to Mrs. P—— stating my destitute condition and imploring her succour; and, till it arrive, I shall keep myself alive on herrings and apples, together with part of a pint of milk, which I share with Leo. He is my great trouble now, though an excellent companion too. But it is not easy to find food for him, unless I give him what is fit for Christians, —though, for that matter, he appears to be as good a Christian as most laymen, or even as some of the clergy. I fried some pouts and eels, yesterday, on purpose for him, for he does not like raw fish. They were very good, but I should hardly have taken the trouble on my own account.

George P—— has just come to say that Mrs. P—— has no bread at present, and is gone away this afternoon, but that she will send me some tomorrow. I mean to have a regular supply from the same source. .... You cannot imagine how much the presence of Leo relieves the feeling of perfect loneliness. He insists upon being in the room with me all the time, except at night, when he sleeps in the shed, and I do not find myself severe enough to drive him out. He accompanies me likewise in all my walks to the village and elsewhere; and, in short, keeps at my heels all the time, except when I go down cellar. Then he stands at the head of the stairs and howls, as if he never expected to see me again. He is evidently impressed with the present solitude of our old abbey, both on his own account and mine, and feels that he may assume a greater degree of intimacy than would be otherwise allowable. He will be easily brought within the old regulations after your return.

P. S. 3 o'clock.—The beef is done!!!

Concord. The old Manse. June 2nd.— ... Everything goes on well with me. At the time of writing my last letter I was without bread. Well, just at supper-time came Mrs. B—— with a large covered dish, which proved to contain a quantity of specially good flapjacks, piping hot, prepared, I suppose, by the fair hands of Miss Martha, or Miss Abby, for Mrs. P—— was not at home. They served me both for supper and breakfast; and I thanked Providence and the young ladies, and compared myself to the prophet fed by ravens,—though the simile does rather more than justice to myself, and not enough to the generous donors of the flapjacks. The next morning, Mrs. P—— herself brought two big loaves of bread, which will last me a week, unless I have some guests to provide for. I have likewise found a hoard of crackers in one of the covered dishes; so that the old castle is sufficiently provisioned to stand a long siege. The corned beef is exquisitely done, and as tender as a young lady's heart, all owing to my skilful cookery; for I consulted Mrs. Hale at every step, and precisely followed her directions. To say the truth, I look upon it as such a masterpiece in its way, that it seems irreverential to eat it. Things on which so much thought and labour are bestowed should surely be immortal. . . . . Leo and I attended divine services this morning in a temple not made with hands. We went to the farthest extremity of Peter's path, and there lay together under an oak, on the verge of the broad meadow.

Salem, June 4th, 1844.— .... I went to George Hillard's office, and he spoke with immitigable resolution of the necessity of my going to dine with Longfellow before returning to Concord; but I have an almost miraculous power of escaping from necessities of this kind. Destiny itself has often been worsted in the attempt to get me out to dinner. Possibly, however, I may go. Afterwards I called on Colonel Hall, who held me long in talk about politics and other sweetmeats. Then I stepped into a book auction, not to buy, but merely to observe, and, after a few moments, who should come in, with a smile as sweet as sugar (though savouring rather of molasses), but, to my horror and petrifaction, —— ——! I anticipated a great deal of bore and botheration; but, through Heaven's mercy, he merely spoke a few words, and left me. This is so unlike his deportment in times past, that I suspect "The Celestial Railroad" must have given him a pique; and, if so, I shall feel as if Providence had sufficiently rewarded me for that pious labour.

In the course of the forenoon I encountered Mr.

Howes in the street. He looked most exceedingly depressed, and, pressing my hand with peculiar emphasis, said that he was in great affliction, having just heard of his son George's death in Cuba. He seemed encompassed and overwhelmed by this misfortune, and walks the street as in a heavy cloud of his own grief, forth from which he extended his hand to meet my grasp. I expressed my sympathy, which I told him I was now the more capable of feeling in a father's suffering, as being myself the father of a little girl,—and, indeed, the being a parent does give one the freedom of a wider range of sorrow as well as of happiness. He again pressed my hand, and left me. . . .

When I got to Salem, there was great joy, as you may suppose. . . . Mother hinted an apprehension that poor baby would be spoilt, whereupon I irreverently observed that, having spoilt her own three children, it was natural for her to suppose that all other parents would do the same; when she averred that it was impossible to spoil such children as E—— and I, because she had never been able to do anything with us. . . . I could hardly convince them that Una had begun to smile so soon. It surprised my mother, though her own children appear to have been bright specimens of babyhood. E—— could walk and talk at nine months old. I do not understand that I was quite such a miracle of precocity, but should think it not impossible, inasmuch as precocious boys are said to make stupid men.

Concord, June 6th.—. . . . Mr. F—— arrived yesterday, and appeared to be in most excellent health, and as happy as the sunshine. About the first thing he did was to wash the dishes; and he is really indefatigable in the kitchen, so that I am quite a gentleman of leisure. Previous to his arrival, I had kindled no fire for four entire days, and had lived all that time on the corned beef, except one day, when Ellery and I went down the river on a fishing excursion. Yesterday, we boiled some lamb, which we shall have cold for dinner to-day. This morning, Mr. F—— fried a sumptuous dish of eels for breakfast. Mrs. P—— continues to be the instrument of Providence, and yesterday sent us a very nice plum-pudding.

I have told Mr. F—— that I shall be engaged in the forenoons, and he is to manage his own occupations and amusements during that time. . . .

Leo, I regret to say, has fallen under suspicion of

a very great crime,—nothing less than murder,—a fowl crime it may well be called, for it is the slaughter of one of Mr. Hayward's hens. He has been seen to chase the hens several times, and the other day one of them was found dead. Possibly he may be innocent, and, as there is nothing but circumstantial evidence, it must be left with his own conscience.

Meantime, Mr. Hayward, or somebody else seems to have given him such a whipping that he is absolutely stiff, and walks about like a rheumatic old gentleman. I am afraid, too, that he is an incorrigible thief. Ellery says he has seen him coming up the avenue with a calf's whole head in his mouth. How he came by it is best known to Leo himself. If he were a dog of fair character, it would be no more than charity to conclude that he had either bought it or had it given to him; but with the other charges against him, it inclines me to great distrust of his moral principles. Be that as it may, he managed his stock of provisions very thriftily,— burying it in the earth, and eating a portion of it whenever he felt an appetite. If he insists upon living by highway robbery, it would be well to make him share his booty with us. . . . .

June 10*th*.—. . . . Mr. F—— is in perfect health, and absolutely in the seventh heaven, and he talks and talks and talks and talks; and I listen and listen and listen with a patience for which, in spite of all my sins, I firmly expect to be admitted to the mansions of the blessed. And there is really a contentment in being able to make this poor, world-worn, hopeless, half-crazy man so entirely comfortable as he seems to be here. He is an admirable cook. We had some roast-veal and a baked rice-pudding on Sunday, really a fine dinner, and cooked in better style than Mary can equal; and George Curtis came to dine with us. Like all male cooks, he is rather expensive, and has a tendency to the consumption of eggs in his various concoctions. . . . . I have had my dreams of splendour; but never expected to arrive at the dignity of keeping a man-cook. At first we had three meals a day, but now only two. . . . .

* * * * *

We dined at Mr. Emerson's the other day, in company with Mr. Hedge. Mr. Bradford has been to see us two or three times. . . . He looks thinner than ever.

[PASSAGES FROM NOTE-BOOKS.]

May 5th, 1850.—I left Portsmouth last Wednesday, at the quarter past twelve, by the Concord Railroad, which at Newcastle unites with the Boston and Maine Railroad about ten miles from Portsmouth. The station at Newcastle is a small wooden building, with one railroad passing on one side, and another on another, and the two crossing each other at right angles. At a little distance stands a black, large, old wooden church, with a square tower, and broken windows, and a great rift through the middle of the roof, all in a stage of dismal ruin and decay. A farmhouse of the old style, with a long, sloping roof, and as black as the church, stands on the opposite side of the road, with its barns; and these are all the buildings in sight of the railroad station. On the Concord rail, in the train of cars, with the locomotive puffing, and blowing off its steam, and making a great bluster in that lonely place, while along the other railroad stretches the desolate track, with the withered weeds growing up betwixt the two lines of iron, all so desolate. And anon you hear a low thunder running along these iron rails; it grows louder; an object is seen afar off; it approaches rapidly, and comes down upon you like fate, swift and inevitable. In a moment, it dashes along in front of the station-house, and comes to a pause, the locomotive hissing and fuming in its eagerness to go on. How much life has come at once into this lonely place? Four or five long cars, each, perhaps, with fifty people in it, reading newspapers, reading pamphlet novels, chattering, sleeping; all this vision of passing life! A moment passes, while the luggage-men are putting on the trunks and packages; then the bell strikes a few times, and away goes the train again, quickly out of sight of those who remain behind, while a solitude of hours again broods over the station-house, which, for an instant, has thus been put in communication with far-off cities, and then remains by itself, with the old, black, ruinous church, and the black old farm-house, both built years and years ago, before railroads were ever dreamed of. Meantime, the passenger, stepping from the solitary station into the train, finds himself in the midst of a new world all in a moment. He rushes out of the solitude into a village; thence, through woods and hills, into a large inland town; beside the Merrimack, which has overflowed its banks, and eddies along, turbid as a vast mud-puddle, sometimes almost laving the doorstep of a house, and with trees standing in the flood half-way up their trunks. Boys, with newspapers to sell, or apples and lozenges; many passengers departing and entering at each new station; the more permanent passenger, with his check or ticket stuck in his hat-band, where the conductor may see it. A party of girls, playing at ball with a young man. Altogether it is a scene of stirring life, with which a person who had been waiting long for the train to come might find it difficult at once to amalgamate himself.

It is a sombre, brooding day, and begins to rain as the cars pass onward. In a little more than two hours we find ourselves in Boston, surrounded by eager hackmen.

Yesterday I went to the Athenæum, and, being received with great courtesy by Mr. Folsom, was shown all over the edifice, from the very bottom to the very top, whence I looked out over Boston. It is an admirable point of view; but, it being an overcast and misty day, I did not get the full advantage of it. The library is in a noble hall, and looks splendidly, with its vista of alcoves. The most remarkable sight, however, was Mr. Hildreth, writing his history of the United States. He sits at a table, at the entrance of one of the alcoves, with his books and papers before him, as quiet and absorbed as he would be in the loneliest study; now consulting an authority, now penning a sentence or a paragraph, without seeming conscious of anything but his subject. It is very curious thus to have a glimpse of a book in process of creation under one's eye. I know not how many hours he sits there; but while I saw him he was a pattern of diligence and unwandering thought. He had taken himself out of the age, and put himself, I suppose, into that about which he was writing. Being deaf, he finds it much the easier to abstract himself. Nevertheless, it is a miracle. He is a thin, middle-aged man, in black, with an intelligent face, rather sensible than scholar-like.

Mr. Folsom accompanied me to call upon Mr. Ticknor, the historian of Spanish literature. He has a fine house, at the corner of Park and Beacon Streets, perhaps the very best position in Boston. A marble hall, a wide and easy staircase, a respectable old man-servant, evidently long at home in the mansion, to admit us. We entered the library, Mr. Folsom considerably in advance, as being familiar with the house; and I heard Mr. Ticknor greet him in friendly tones, their scholar-like and bibliographical pursuits, I suppose, bringing them into frequent conjunction.

Then I was introduced, and received with great distinction, but yet without any ostentatious flourish of courtesy. Mr. Ticknor has a great head, and his hair is grey or greyish. You recognize in him at once the man who knows the world, the scholar, too, which probably is his more distinctive character, though a little more under the surface. He was in his slippers; a volume of his book was open on a table, and apparently he had been engaged in revising or annotating it. His library is a stately and beautiful room for a private dwelling, and itself looks large and rich. The fire-place has a white marble frame about it, sculptured with figures and reliefs. Over it hung a portrait of Sir Walter Scott, a copy, I think, of the one that represents him in Melrose Abbey.

Mr. Ticknor was most kind in his alacrity to solve the point on which Mr. Folsom, in my behalf, had consulted him (as to whether there had been any English translation of the " Tales of Cervantes"); and most liberal in his offers of books from his library. Certainly, he is a fine example of a generous-principled scholar, anxious to assist the human intellect in its efforts and researches. Methinks he must have spent a happy life (as happiness goes among mortals), writing his great three-volumed book for twenty years; writing it, not for bread, nor with any uneasy desire of fame, but only with a purpose to achieve something true and enduring. He is, I apprehend, a man of great cultivation and refinement, and with quite substance enough to be polished and refined, without being worn too thin in the process—a man of society. He related a singular story of an attempt of his to become acquainted with me years ago, when he mistook my kinsman Eben for me.

At half-past four, I went to Mr. Thompson's, the artist who has requested to paint my picture. This was the second sitting. The portrait looked dimly out from the canvas, as from a cloud, with something that I could recognize as my outline, but no strong resemblance as yet. I have had three portraits taken before this,—an oil picture, a miniature, and a crayon sketch, neither of them satisfactory to those most familiar with my physiognomy. In fact, there is no such thing as a true portrait; they are all delusions, and I never saw any two alike, nor hardly any two that I would recognize, merely by the portraits themselves, as being of the same man. A bust has more reality. This artist is a man of thought, and with no mean idea of his art; a Swedenborgian, or, as he prefers to call it, a member of the New Church; and

I have generally found something marked in men who adopt that faith. He had painted a good picture of Bryant. He seems to me to possess truth in himself, and to aim at it in his artistic endeavours.

May 6th.—This morning it is an easterly rain, (south-easterly I should say just now at twelve o'clock,) and I went at nine, by appointment, to sit for my picture. The artist painted awhile; but soon found that he had not so much light as was desirable, and complained that his tints were as muddy as the weather. Further sitting was therefore postponed till to-morrow at eleven. It will be a good picture; but I see no assurance, as yet, of the likeness. An artist's apartment is always very interesting to me, with its pictures, finished and unfinished; its little fancies in the pictorial way,—as here two sketches of children among flowers and foliage, representing Spring and Summer, Winter and Autumn being yet to come out of the artist's mind; the portraits of his wife and children; here a clergyman, there a poet; here a woman with the stamp of reality upon her, there a feminine conception which we feel not to have existed. There was an infant Christ, or rather a child Christ, not unbeautiful but scarcely divine. I love the odour of paint in an artist's room; his palette and all his other tools have a mysterious charm for me. The pursuit has always interested my imagination more than any other, and I remember, before having my first portrait taken, there was a great bewitchery in the idea, as if it were a magic process. Even now, it is not without interest to me.

I left Mr. Thompson before ten, and took my way through the sloppy streets to the Athenæum, where I looked over the newspapers and periodicals, and found two of my old stories ("Peter Goldthwaite" and "The Shaker Bridal") published as original in the last *London Metropolitan!* The English are much more unscrupulous and dishonest pirates than ourselves. However, if they are poor enough to perk themselves in such false feathers as these, Heaven help them! I glanced over the stories, and they seemed painfully cold and dull. It is the more singular that these should be so published, inasmuch as the whole book was republished in London, only a few months ago. Mr. Fields tells me that two publishers in London had advertised "The Scarlet Letter" as in press, each book at a shilling.

*   *   *   *   *

Certainly life is made much more tolerable, and man respects himself far more, when he takes his meals with a certain degree of order and state. There should be a sacred law in these matters; and, as consecrating the whole business, the preliminary prayer is a good and real ordinance. The advance of man from a savage and animal state may be as well measured by his mode and morality of dining, as by any other circumstance. At Mr. Fields's, soon after entering the house, I heard the brisk and cheerful notes of a canary bird, singing with great vivacity, and making its voice echo through the large rooms. It was very pleasant, at the close of the rainy, east-windy day, and seemed to fling sunshine through the dwelling.

May 7th.—I did not go out yesterday afternoon, but after tea I went to Parker's. The drinking and smoking shop is no bad place to see one kind of life. The front apartment is for drinking. The door opens into Court Square, and is denoted, usually, by some choice specimens of dainties exhibited in the windows, or hanging beside the door-post; as, for instance, a pair of canvas-back ducks, distinguishable by their delicately mottled feathers; an admirable cut of raw beefsteak; a ham, ready boiled, and with curious figures traced in spices on its outward fat; a half, or perchance the whole, of a large salmon, when in season; a bunch of partridges, &c. &c. A screen stands directly before the door, so as to conceal the interior from an outside barbarian. At the counter stand, at almost all hours,—certainly at all hours when I have chanced to observe,—tipplers, either taking a solitary glass, or treating all round, veteran topers, flashy young men, visitors from the country, the various petty officers connected with the law, whom the vicinity of the Court-house brings hither. Chiefly, they drink plain liquors, gin, brandy, or whisky, sometimes a Tom and Jerry, a gin cocktail (which the bar-tender makes artistically, tossing it in a large parabola from one tumbler to another, until fit for drinking), a brandy-smash, and numerous other concoctions. All this toping goes forward with little or no apparent exhilaration of spirits; nor does this seem to be the object sought,—it being either, I imagine, to create a titillation of the coats of the stomach and a general sense of invigoration, without affecting the brain. Very seldom does a man grow wild and unruly.

The inner room is hung round with pictures and engravings of various kinds,—a painting of a premium ox, a lithograph of a Turk and of a Turkish lady, ... and various showily engraved tailors' advertisements, and other shop bills ; among them all, a small painting of a drunken toper, sleeping on a bench beside the grog-shop,—a ragged, half-hatless, bloated, red-nosed, jolly, miserable-looking devil, very well done, and strangely suitable to the room in which it hangs. Round the walls are placed some half-a-dozen marble-topped tables, and a centre-table in the midst ; most of them strewn with theatrical and other show-bills ; and the large theatre bills, with their type of gigantic solidity and blackness, hung against the walls.

Last evening, when I entered, there was one guest somewhat overcome with liquor, and slumbering with his chair tipped against one of the marble tables. In the course of a quarter of an hour, he roused himself (a plain, middle-aged man), and went out with rather an unsteady step, and a hot, red face. One or two others were smoking, and looking over the papers, or glancing at a play-bill. From the centre of the ceiling descended a branch with two gas-burners, which sufficiently illuminated every corner of the room. Nothing is so remarkable in these bar-rooms and drinking-places, as the perfect order that prevails :

if a man gets drunk, it is no otherwise perceptible than by his going to sleep, or his inability to walk.

Pacing the sidewalk in front of this grog-shop of Parker's (or sometimes, on cold and rainy days, taking his station inside), there is generally to be observed an elderly ragamuffin, in a dingy and battered hat, an old surtout, and a more than shabby general aspect; a thin face and red nose, a patch over one eye, and the other half drowned in moisture. He leans in a slightly stooping posture on a stick, forlorn and silent, addressing nobody, but fixing his one moist eye on you with a certain intentness. He is a man who has been in decent circumstances at some former period of his life, but, falling into decay (perhaps by dint of too frequent visits at Parker's bar), he now haunts about the place, as a ghost haunts the spot where he was murdered, "to collect his rents," as Parker says,—that is, to catch an occasional ninepence from some charitable acquaintances, or a glass of liquor at the bar. The word "ragamuffin" which I have used above, does not accurately express the man, because there is a sort of shadow or delusion of respectability about him, and a sobriety too, and a kind of decency in his groggy and red-nosed destitution.

Underground, beneath the drinking and smoking-rooms, is Parker's eating-hall, extending all the way to Court Street. All sorts of good eating may be had there, and a gourmand may feast at what expense he will.

I take an interest in all the nooks and crannies and every development of cities; so here I try to make a description of the view from the back windows of a house in the centre of Boston, at which I now glance in the intervals of writing. The view is bounded, at perhaps thirty yards' distance, by a row of opposite brick dwellings, standing, I think, on Temple Place; houses of the better order, with tokens of genteel families visible in all the rooms betwixt the basements and the attic windows in the roof; plate-glass in the rear drawing-rooms, flower-pots in some of the windows of the upper storeys. Occasionally, a lady's figure, either seated or appearing with a flitting grace, or dimly manifest farther within the obscurity of the room. A balcony, with a wrought-iron fence running along under the row of drawing-room windows, above the basement. In the space betwixt the opposite row of dwellings and that in which I am situated, are the low out-houses of the above-described houses, with flat roofs; or solid brick walls, with walks on them, and high railings, for the convenience of the washerwomen in hanging out their clothes. In the intervals are grass-plots, already green, because so sheltered; and fruit-trees, now beginning to put forth their leaves, and one of them, a cherry-tree, almost in full blossom. Birds flutter and sing among these trees. I should judge it a good site for the growth of delicate fruit; for, quite enclosed on all sides by houses, the blighting winds cannot molest the trees. They have sunshine on them a good part of the day, though the shadow must come early, and I suppose there is a rich soil about the roots. I see grape-vines clambering against one wall, and also peeping over another, where the main body of the vine is invisible to me. In another place, a frame is erected for a grape-vine, and probably it will produce as rich clusters as the vines of Madeira, here in the heart of the city, in this little spot of fructifying earth, while the thunder of wheels rolls about it on every side. The trees are not all fruit-trees. One pretty well-grown buttonwood-tree aspires upward above the roofs of the houses. In the full verdure of summer, there will be quite a mass or curtain of foliage between the hither and the thither row of houses.

Afternoon.—At eleven, I went to give Mr. Thompson a sitting for my picture. I like the painter. He seems to reverence his art and to aim at truth in it, as I said before ; a man of gentle disposition, too, and simplicity of life and character. I seated myself in the pictorial chair, with the only light in the room descending upon me from a high opening, almost at the ceiling, the rest of the sole window being shuttered. He began to work, and we talked in an idle and desultory way,—neither of us feeling very conversable,—which he attributed to the atmosphere, it being a bright, west-windy, bracing day. We talked about the pictures of Christ, and how inadequate and untrue they are. He said he thought artists should attempt only to paint child-Christs, human powers being inadequate to the task of painting such purity and holiness in a manly development. Then he said that an idea of a picture had occurred to him that morning, while reading a chapter in the New Testament,—how "they parted his garments among them, and for his vesture did cast lots." His picture was to represent the soldier to whom the garment without a seam had fallen, after taking it home and examining it, and becoming impressed with a sense of the former wearer's holiness. I do not quite see how he would make such a picture tell its own story; but I find the idea suggestive to my own mind, and I think I could make something of it. We talked of physiognomy and impressions of character,—first impressions,—and how apt they are to come aright in the face of the closest subsequent observation.

There were several visitors in the course of the sitting, one a gentleman, a connection from the country, with whom the artist talked about family matters and personal affairs,—observing on the poorness of his own business, and that he had thoughts of returning to New York. I wish he would meet with better success. Two or three ladies also looked in. Meanwhile, Mr. Thompson had been painting with more and more eagerness, casting quick, keen glances at me, and then making hasty touches on the picture, as if to secure with his brush what he had caught with his eye. He observed that he was just getting interested in the work, and I could recognize the feeling that was in him as akin to what I have experienced myself in the glow of composition. Nevertheless, he seemed able to talk about foreign matters through it all. He continued to paint in this rapid way up to the moment of closing the sitting; when he took the canvas from the easel, without giving me time to mark what progress he had made, as he did the last time.

The artist is middle-sized, thin, a little stooping, with a quick, nervous movement. He has black hair, not thick, a beard under his chin, a small head, but well-developed forehead, black eyebrows, eyes keen, but kindly, and a dark face, not indicating robust health, but agreeable in its expression. His voice is gentle and sweet, and such as comes out from amidst refined feelings. He dresses very simply and unpictorially in a grey frock or sack, and does not seem to think of making a picture of himself in his own person.

At dinner to-day there was a young Frenchman, whom —— befriended a year or so ago, when he had not another friend in America, and obtained employment for him in a large dry-goods establishment. He is a young man of eighteen or thereabouts, with smooth black hair, neatly dressed; his face showing a good disposition, but with nothing of intellect or character. It is funny to think of this poor little Frenchman, a Parisian too, eating our most un-French victuals,— our beefsteaks, and roasts, and various homely puddings and hams, and all things most incongruent to his hereditary stomach; but nevertheless he eats most cheerfully and uncomplainingly. He has not a large measure of French vivacity, never rattles, never dances, nor breaks into ebullitions of mirth and song; on the contrary, I have never known a youth of his age more orderly and decorous. He is kindhearted and grateful, and evinces his gratitude to the mother of the family and to his benefactress by occasional presents, not trifling when measured by his small emolument of five dollars per week. Just at this time he is confined to his room by indisposition, caused, it is suspected, by a spree on Sunday last. Our gross Saxon orgies would soon be the ruin of his French constitution.

A thought to-day. Great men need to be lifted upon the shoulders of the whole world, in order to conceive their great ideas or perform their great deeds. That is, there must be an atmosphere of greatness round about them. A hero cannot be a hero unless in an heroic world.

May 8th.—I went last evening to the National Theatre to see a pantomime. It was Jack the Giant-

Killer, and somewhat heavy and tedious. The audience was more noteworthy than the play. The theatre itself is for the middling and lower classes, and I had not taken my seat in the most aristocratic part of the house; so that I found myself surrounded chiefly by young sailors, Hanover Street shopmen, mechanics, and other people of that class. It is wonderful! the difference that exists in the personal aspect and dress, and no less in the manners, of people in this quarter of the city, as compared with other parts of it.

One would think that Oak Hall should give a common garb and air to the great mass of the Boston population; but it seems not to be so; and perhaps what is most singular is, that the natural make of the men has a conformity and suitableness to the dress. Glazed caps and Palo Alto hats were much worn. It is a pity that this picturesque and comparatively graceful hat should not have been generally adopted, instead of falling to the exclusive use of a rowdy class.

In the next box to me were two young women, with an infant, but to which of them appertaining I could not at first discover. One was a large, plump girl, with a heavy face, a snub nose, coarse-looking, but good-natured, and with no traits of evil,—save, indeed, that she had on the vilest gown of dirty white cotton, so pervadingly dingy that it was white no longer, as it seemed to me. The sleeves were short, and ragged at the borders, and her shawl, which she took off on account of the heat, was old and faded,— the shabbiest and dirtiest dress that I ever saw a woman wear. Yet she was plump, and looked comfortable in body and mind. I imagine that she must have had a better dress at home, but had come to the theatre extemporaneously, and, not going to the dress circle, considered her ordinary gown good enough for the occasion. The other girl seemed as young or younger than herself. She was small, with a particularly intelligent and pleasant face, not handsome, perhaps, but as good or better than if it were. It was mobile with whatever sentiment chanced to be in her mind, as quick and vivacious a face in its movements as I have ever seen; cheerful, too, and indicative of a sunny, though I should think it might be a hasty, temper. She was dressed in a dark gown (chintz, I suppose the women call it), a good, homely dress, proper enough for the fireside, but a strange one to appear in at a theatre. Both these girls appeared to enjoy themselves very much,—the large and heavy one in her own duller mode; the smaller manifesting her interest by gestures, pointing at the stage, and with so vivid a talk of countenance that it was precisely as if she had spoken. She was not a brunette, and this made the vivacity of her expression the more agreeable. Her companion, on the other hand, was so dark, that I rather suspected her to have a tinge of African blood.

There were two men who seemed to have some connection with these girls,—one an elderly, grey-headed personage, well-stricken in liquor, talking loudly and foolishly, but good-humouredly; the other a young man, sober, and doing his best to keep his elder friend quiet. The girls seemed to give themselves no uneasiness about the matter. Both the men wore Palo Alto hats. I could not make out whether either of the men were the father of the child, though I was inclined to set it down as a family party.

As the play went on, the house became crowded and oppressively warm, and the poor little baby grew dark red, or purple almost, with the uncomfortable heat in its small body. It must have been accustomed to discomfort, and have concluded it to be the condition of mortal life, else it never would have remained so quiet. Perhaps it had been quieted with a sleeping-potion. The two young women were not negligent of it; but passed it to and fro between them, each willingly putting herself to inconvenience for the sake of tending it. But I really feared it might die in some kind of a fit, so hot was the theatre, so purple with heat, yet strangely quiet, was the child. I was glad to hear it cry at last; but it did not cry with any great rage and vigour, as it should, but in a stupid kind of way. Hereupon the smaller of the two girls, after a little inefficacious dandling, at once settled the question of maternity by nursing her baby. Children must be hard to kill, however injudicious the treatment. The two girls and their cavaliers remained till nearly the close of the play. I should like well to know who they are,—of what condition in life, and whether reputable as members of the class to which they belong. My own judgment is that they are so. Throughout the evening, drunken young sailors kept stumbling into and out of the boxes, calling to one another from different parts of the house, shouting to the performers, and singing the burden of songs. It was a scene of life in the rough.

May 14*th*.—A stable opposite the house,—an old

wooden construction, low, in three distinct parts; the centre being the stable proper, where the horses are kept, and with a chamber over it for the hay. On one side is the department for chaises and carriages; on the other, the little office where the books are kept. In the interior region of the stable everything is dim and undefined,—half-traceable outlines of stalls, sometimes the shadowy aspect of a horse. Generally a groom is dressing a horse at the stable door, with a care and accuracy that leave no part of the animal unvisited by the currycomb and brush; the horse, meanwhile, evidently enjoying it, but sometimes, when the more sensitive parts are touched, giving a half-playful kick with his hind legs, and a little neigh. If the men bestowed half as much care on their own personal cleanliness, they would be all the better and healthier men therefor. They appear to be busy men, these stablers, yet have a lounging way with them, as if indolence were somehow diffused through their natures. The apparent head of the establishment is a sensible, thoughtful-looking, large-featured and homely man, past the middle age, clad rather shabbily in grey, stooping somewhat, and without any smartness about him. There is a groom, who seems to be a very comfortable kind of personage,—

a man of forty-five or thereabouts (R. W. Emerson says he was one of his schoolmates), but not looking so old ; corpulent, not to say fat, with a white frock, which his goodly bulk almost fills, enveloping him from neck nearly to ankles. On his head he wears a cloth cap of a jockey shape ; his pantaloons are turned up an inch or two at bottom, and he wears brogans on his feet. His hair, as may be seen when he takes off his cap to wipe his brow, is black and in perfect preservation, with not exactly a curl, yet a vivacious and elastic kind of twist in it. His face is fresh-coloured, comfortable, sufficiently vivid in expression, not at all dimmed by his fleshly exuberance, because the man possesses vigour enough to carry it off. His bodily health seems perfect ; so, indeed, does his moral and intellectual. He is very active and assiduous in his duties, currycombing and rubbing down the horses with alacrity and skill ; and, when not otherwise occupied, you may see him talking jovially with chance acquaintances, or observing what is going forward in the street. If a female acquaintance happens to pass, he touches his jockey cap, and bows, accomplishing this courtesy with a certain smartness that proves him a man of the world. Whether it be his greater readiness to talk, or the wisdom of what he says, he seems usually to be the centre talker of the group. It is very pleasant to see such an image of earthly comfort as this. A fat man who feels his flesh as a disease and encumbrance, and on whom it presses so as to make him melancholy with dread of apoplexy, and who moves heavily under the burden of himself,—such a man is a doleful and disagreeable object. But if he have vivacity enough to pervade all his earthiness, and bodily force enough to move lightly under it, and if it be not too unmeasured to have a trimness and briskness in it, then it is good and wholesome to look at him.

In the background of the house, a cat, occasionally stealing along on the roofs of the low outhouses; descending a flight of wooden steps into the brick area : investigating the shed, and entering all dark and secret places; cautious, circumspect, as if in search of something; noiseless, attentive to every noise. Moss grows on spots of the roof; there are little boxes of earth here and there, with plants in them. The grass-plots appertaining to each of the houses whose rears are opposite ours (standing in Temple Place) are perhaps ten or twelve feet broad, and three times as long. Here and there is a large, painted garden-pot, half buried in earth. Besides the large trees in blossom, there are little ones, probably of last year's setting out. Early in the day chambermaids are seen hanging the bedclothes out of the upper windows; at the window of the basement of the same house I see a woman ironing. Were I a solitary prisoner, I should not doubt to find occupation of deep interest for my whole day in watching only one of the houses. One house seems to be quite shut up; all the blinds in the three windows of each of the four storeys being closed, although in the roof-windows of the attic storey the curtains are hung carelessly upward, instead of being drawn. I think the house is empty, perhaps for the summer. The visible side of the whole row of houses is now in the shade,—they looking towards, I should say, the southwest. Later in the day, they are wholly covered with sunshine, and continue so through the afternoon; and at evening the sunshine slowly withdraws upward, gleams aslant upon the windows, perches on the chimneys, and so disappears. The upper part of the spire and the weathercock of the Park Street Church appear over one of the houses, looking as if it were close behind. It shows the wind to be east now. At one of the windows of the third storey sits a woman in a coloured dress, diligently sowing on something white. She sews, not like a lady, but with an occupational air. Her dress, I observe, on closer observation, is a kind of loose morning sack, with, I think, a silky gloss on it; and she seems to have a silver comb in her hair,—no, this latter item is a mistake. Sheltered as the space is between the two rows of houses, a puff of the east wind finds its way in, and shakes off some of the withering blossoms from the cherry-trees.

Quiet as the prospect is, there is a continual and near thunder of wheels proceeding from Washington Street. In a building not far off, there is a hall for exhibitions; and sometimes, in the evenings, loud music is heard from it; or, if a diorama be shown (that of Bunker Hill, for instance, or the burning of Moscow), an immense racket of imitative cannon and musketry.

May 16th.—It has been an easterly rain yesterday and to-day, with occasional lightings up, and then a heavy downfall of the gloom again.

Scenes out of the rear windows,—the glistening roof of the opposite houses; the chimneys, now and then choked with their own smoke, which a blast drives down their throats. The church-spire has a mist about it. Once this morning a solitary dove came and alighted on the peak of an attic window, and looked down into the areas, remaining in this position a considerable time. Now it has taken a flight, and alighted on the roof of this house, directly over the window at which I sit, so that I can look up and see its head and beak, and the tips of its claws. The roofs of the low out-houses are black with moisture; the gutters are full of water, and there is a little puddle where there is a place for it in the hollow of a board. On the grass-plot are strewn the fallen blossoms of the cherry-tree, and over the scene broods a parallelogram of sombre sky. Thus it will be all day as it was yesterday; and, in the evening, one window after another will be lighted up in the drawing-rooms. Through the white curtains may be seen the gleam of an astral lamp, like a fixed star. In the basement rooms, the work of the kitchen going forward; in the upper chambers, here and there a light.

In the bar-room, a large oval basin let into the counter, with a brass tube rising from the centre, out of which gushes continually a miniature fountain, and descends in a soft, gentle, never-ceasing rain into the basin, where swim a company of gold-fishes. Some of them gleam brightly in their golden armour; others have a dull white aspect, going through some process of transformation. One would think that the atmosphere, continually filled with tobacco-smoke, might impregnate the water unpleasantly for the scaly people; but then it is continually flowing away and being renewed. And what if some toper should be seized with the freak of emptying his glass of gin or brandy into the basin,—would the fishes die or merely get jolly?

I saw, for a wonder, a man pretty drunk at Parker's the other evening,—a well-dressed man, of not ungentlemanly aspect. He talked loudly and foolishly, but in good phrases, with a great flow of language, and he was no otherwise impertinent than in addressing his talk to strangers. Finally, after sitting a long time staring steadfastly across the room in silence, he arose and staggered away as best he might, only showing his very drunken state when he attempted to walk.

Old acquaintances,—a gentleman whom I knew ten years ago, brisk, active, vigorous, with a kind of fire of physical well-being and cheerful spirits glowing through him. Now, after a course, I presume, of rather free living, pale, thin, oldish, with a grave and care- or pain-worn brow,—yet still lively and cheerful in his accost, though with something invincibly saddened in his tones. Another, formerly commander of a revenue vessel,—a man of splendid epaulets and very aristocratic equipment and demeanour; now out of service and without position, and changed into a brandy-burnt and rowdyish sort of personage. He seemed as if he might still be a gentleman if he would; but his manners show a desperate state of mind by their familiarity, recklessness, the lack of any hedge of reserve about himself, while still he is evidently a man of the world, accustomed to good society. He has latterly, I think, been in the Russian service, and would very probably turn pirate on fair occasion.

Lenox, July 14th.—The tops of the chestnut-trees have a whitish appearance, they being, I suppose, in bloom. Red raspberries are just through the season.

*   *   *   *   *

Language,—human language,—after all, is but little better than the croak and cackle of fowls and other utterances of brute nature,—sometimes not so adequate.

July 16*th*.—The tops of the chestnut-trees are peculiarly rich, as if a more luscious sunshine were falling on them than anywhere else. "Whitish," as above, don't express it.

The queer gestures and sounds of a hen looking about for a place to deposit her egg; her self-important gait; the sideway turn of her head and cock of her eye, as she prys into one and another nook, croaking all the while,—evidently with the idea that the egg in question is the most important thing that has been brought to pass since the world began. A speckled black-and-white and tufted hen of ours does it to most ludicrous perfection; and there is something laughably womanish in it too.

July 25*th*.—As I sit in my study, with the windows open, the occasional incident of the visit of some winged creature,—wasp, hornet, or bee,—entering out of the warm sunny atmosphere, soaring round the room in large sweeps, then buzzing against the glass, as not satisfied with the place, and desirous of getting out. Finally, the joyous, uprising curve with which, coming to the open part of the window, it emerges into the cheerful glow of the outside.

August 4th.—Dined at hotel with J. T. Fields and wife. Afternoon, drove with them to Pittsfield and called on Dr. Holmes.

August 5th.—Drove with Fields and his wife to Stockbridge, being thereto invited by Mr. Field of Stockbridge, in order to ascend Monument Mountain. Found at Mr. Field's Dr. Holmes and Mr. Duyckink of New York; also Mr. Cornelius Matthews and Herman Melville. Ascended the mountain; that is to say, Mrs. Fields and Miss Jenny Field, Mr. Field and Mr. Fields, Dr. Holmes, Messrs. Duyckink, Matthews, Melville, Mr. Henry Sedgewick, and I, and were caught in a shower. Dined at Mr. Field's. Afternoon, under guidance of J. T. Headley, the party scrambled through the ice-glen.

August 7th.—Messrs. Duyckink, Matthews, Melville, and Melville, junior, called in the forenoon. Gave them a couple of bottles of Mr. Mansfield's champagne, and walked down to the lake with them. At twilight Mr. Edwin P. Whipple and wife called.

August 8th.—Mr. and Mrs. Whipple took tea with us.

August 12*th.*—Seven chickens hatched. J. T. Headley and brother called. Eight chickens.

August 19*th.*—Monument Mountain in the early sunshine; its base enveloped in mist, parts of which are floating in the sky, so that the great hill looks really as if it were founded on a cloud. Just emerging from the mist is seen a yellow field of rye, and, above that, forest.

August 21*st.* — Eight more chickens hatched. Ascended a mountain with my wife; a beautiful, mellow, autumnal sunshine.

August 24*th.*—In the afternoons, nowadays, this valley in which I dwell seems like a vast basin filled with golden sunshine as with wine.

August 31*st.*—J. R. Lowell called in the evening.

September 1*st.*—Mr. and Mrs. Lowell called in the forenoon, on their way to Stockbridge or Lebanon to meet Miss Bremer.

September 2*nd.* — " When I grow up," quoth

J——, in illustration of the might to which he means to attain,—"when I grow up I shall be two men."

September 3rd.—Foliage of maples begins to change. Julian, after picking up a handful of autumnal maple-leaves the other day,—"Look, papa, here's a bunch of fire!"

September 7th.—In a wood, a heap or pile of logs and sticks, that had been cut for firewood, and piled up square, in order to be carted away to the house when convenience served,—or, rather, to be sledded in sleighing time. But the moss had accumulated on them, and leaves falling over them from year to year, and decaying, a kind of soil had quite covered them, although the softened outline of the wood-pile was perceptible in the green mound. It was perhaps fifty years—perhaps more—since the woodman had cut and piled those logs and sticks, intending them for his winter fires. But he probably needs no fire now. There was something strangely interesting in this simple circumstance. Imagine the long-dead woodman, and his long-dead wife and family, and the old man who was a little child when the wood was cut, coming back from their graves, and trying to make a fire with this mossy fuel.

September 19*th.*—Lying by the lake yesterday afternoon, with my eyes shut, while the waves and sunshine were playing together on the water, the quick glimmer of the wavelets was perceptible through my closed eyelids.

October 13*th.*—A windy day, with wind northwest, cool, with a prevalence of dull grey clouds over the sky, but with brief, quick glimpses of sunshine.

The foliage having its autumn hues, Monument Mountain looks like a headless sphinx, wrapped in a rich Persian shawl. Yesterday, through a diffused mist, with the sun shining on it, it had the aspect of burnished copper. The sun-gleams on the hills are peculiarly magnificent just in these days.

One of the children, drawing a cow on the blackboard, says, "I'll kick this leg out a little more,"— a very happy energy of expression, completely identifying herself with the cow; or perhaps, as the cow's creator, conscious of full power over its movements.

October 14*th*.—The brilliancy of the foliage has passed its acme; and indeed it has not been so magnificent this season as in some others, owing to the gradual approaches of cooler weather, and there having been slight frosts instead of severe ones. There is still a shaggy richness on the hillsides.

October 16*th*.—A morning mist, filling up the whole length and breadth of the valley betwixt my house and Monument Mountain, the summit of the mountain emerging. The mist reaches almost to my window, so dense as to conceal everything, except that near its hither boundary a few ruddy or yellow tree-tops appear, glorified by the early sunshine, as is likewise the whole mist-cloud.

There is a glen between this house and the lake, through which winds a little brook with pools and tiny waterfalls over the great roots of trees. The glen is deep and narrow, and filled with trees; so that, in the summer, it is all a dense shadow of obscurity. Now, the foliage of the trees being almost entirely a golden yellow, instead of being full of shadow, the glen is absolutely full of sunshine, and its depths are more brilliant than the open plain or the mountain-tops. The trees are sunshine, and, many of the golden leaves being freshly fallen, the glen is strewn with sunshine, amid which winds and gurgles the bright, dark little brook.

December 1st.—I saw a dandelion in bloom near the lake.

December 19th.—If the world were crumbled to the finest dust, and scattered through the universe, there would not be an atom of the dust for each star.

" Generosity is the flower of justice."

The print in blood of a naked foot to be traced through the street of a town.

Sketch of a personage with the malignity of a witch, and doing the mischief attributed to one,—but by natural means ; breaking off love-affairs, teaching children vices, ruining men of wealth, &c.

Ladislaus, King of Naples, besieging the city of Florence, agreed to show mercy, provided the inhabitants would deliver to him a certain virgin of famous beauty, the daughter of a physician of the city. When she was sent to the king, every one contributing something to adorn her in the richest manner, her father gave her a perfumed handkerchief, at that time a universal decoration, richly wrought. This handkerchief was poisoned with his utmost art. . . . and they presently died in one another's arms.

Of a bitter satirist,—of Swift, for instance,— it might be said, that the person or thing on which his satire fell shrivelled up as if the Devil had spit on it.

The Fount of Tears,—a traveller to discover it,— and other similar localities.

Benvenuto Cellini saw a Salamander in the household fire. It was shown him by his father, in childhood.

For the virtuoso's collection,—the pen with which Faust signed away his salvation, with the drop of blood dried in it.

An article on newspaper advertisements, — a

country newspaper, methinks, rather than a city one.

An eating-house, where all the dishes served out, even to the bread and salt, shall be poisoned with the adulterations that are said to be practised. Perhaps Death himself might be the cook.

Personify the century,—talk of its present middle age,—of its youth,—and its adventures and prospects.

An uneducated countryman, supposing he had a live frog in his stomach, applied himself to the study of medicine in order to find a cure for this disease; and he became a profound physician. Thus misfortune, physical or moral, may be the means of educating and elevating us.

Mather's *Manduction and Ministerium*,—or "Directions for a candidate" for the ministry,—with the autographs of four successive clergymen in it, all of them, at one time or another, residents of the old Manse,—Daniel Bliss, 1734; William Emerson, 1770; Ezra Ripley, 1781; and Samuel Ripley, son of the preceding. The book, according to a Latin memorandum, was sold to Daniel Bliss by Daniel Bremer, who, I suppose, was another student of divinity. Printed at Boston "for Thomas Hancock, and sold at his shop in Ann St. near the Draw Bridge, 1726." William Emerson was son-in-law of Daniel Bliss. Ezra Ripley married the widow of said William Emerson, and Samuel Ripley was their son.

Mrs. Prescott has an ox whose visage bears a strong resemblance to Daniel Webster,—a majestic brute.

The spells of witches have the power of producing meats and viands that have the appearance of a sumptuous feast, which the Devil furnishes. But a Divine Providence seldom permits the meat to be good, but it has generally some bad taste or smell,— mostly wants salt,—and the feast is often without bread.

An article on cemeteries, with fantastic ideas of monuments; for instance, a sun-dial;—a large, wide carved stone chair, with some such motto as "Rest and Think," and others, facetious or serious.

"Mamma, I see a part of your smile,"—a child to her mother, whose mouth was partly covered by her hand.

"The syrup of my bosom,"—an improvisation of a little girl, addressed to an imaginary child.

"The wind-turn," the "lightning-catch,"—a child's phrases for weathercock and lightning-rod.

"Where's the man-mountain of these Lilliputs?" cried a little boy, as he looked at a small engraving of the Greeks getting into the wooden horse.

When the sun shines brightly on the new snow, we discover ranges of hills, miles away towards the south, which we have never seen before.

To have the North Pole for a fishing-pole, and the Equinoctial Line for a fishing-line.

If we consider the lives of the lower animals, we shall see in them a close parallelism to those of mortals;—toil, struggle, danger, privation, mingled with glimpses of peace and ease; enmity, affection, a continual hope of bettering themselves, although their objects lie at less distance before them than ours can do. Thus, no argument for the imperfect character of our existence and its delusory promises, and its apparent injustice, can be drawn in reference to our immortality, without, in a degree, being applicable to our brute brethren.

Lenox, February 12*th*, 1851.—A walk across the lake with Una. A heavy rain, some days ago, has melted a good deal of the snow on the intervening descent between our house and the lake; but many drifts, depths, and levels yet remain; and there is a frozen crust, sufficient to bear a man's weight, and very slippery. Adown the slopes there are tiny rivulets, which exist only for the winter. Bare, brown spaces of grass here and there, but still so infrequent as only to diversify the scene a little. In the woods, rocks emerging, and, where there is a slope immediately towards the lake, the snow is pretty much gone, and we see partridge-berries frozen, and outer shells of walnuts, and chestnut-burrs, heaped or scattered among the roots of the trees. The walnut-husks mark the place where the boys, after nutting, sat down to clear the walnuts of their outer shell.

The various species of pine look exceedingly brown just now,—less beautiful than those trees which shed their leaves. An oak-tree, with almost all its brown foliage still rustling on it. We clamber down the bank, and step upon the frozen lake. It was snow-covered for a considerable time; but the rain overspread it with a surface of water, or imperfectly melted snow, which is now hard frozen again; and the thermometer having been frequently below zero, I suppose the ice may be four or five feet thick. Frequently there are great cracks across it, caused, I suppose, by the air beneath, and giving an idea of greater firmness than if there were no cracks; round holes, which have been hewn in the marble pavement by fishermen, and are now frozen over again, looking darker than the rest of the surface; spaces where the snow was more imperfectly dissolved than elsewhere; little crackling spots, where a thin surface of ice, over the real mass, crumples beneath one's foot; the track of a line of footsteps, most of them vaguely formed, but some quite perfectly, where a person passed across the lake, while its surface was in a state of slush, but which are now as hard as adamant, and remind one of the traces discovered by geologists in rocks that hardened thousands of ages ago. It seems as if the person passed when the lake was in an intermediate state between ice and water. In one spot some pine boughs, which somebody had cut and heaped there for an unknown purpose. In the centre of the lake, we see the surrounding hills in a new attitude, this being a basin in the midst of them. Where they are covered with wood, the aspect is gray or black; then there are bare slopes of unbroken snow, the outlines and indentations being much more hardly and firmly defined than in summer. We went southward across the lake, directly towards Monument Mountain, which reposes, as I said, like a headless sphinx. Its prominences, projections, and roughnesses are very evident; and it does not present a smooth and placid front, as when the grass is green and the trees in leaf. At one end, too, we are sensible of precipitous descents, black and shaggy with the forest that is likely always to grow there; and, in one streak, a headlong sweep downward of snow. We just set our feet on the farther shore, and then immediately returned, facing the north-west wind, which blew very sharply against us.

After landing, we came homeward, tracing up the little brook so far as it lay in our course. It was considerably swollen, and rushed fleetly on its course between overhanging banks of snow and ice, from which depended adamantine icicles. The little waterfalls with which we had impeded it in the summer and autumn, could do no more than form a large ripple, so much greater was the volume of water. In some places the crust of frozen snow made a bridge quite over the brook; so that you only knew it was there by its brawling sound beneath.

The sunsets of winter are incomparably splendid, and when the ground is covered with snow, no brilliancy of tint expressible by words can come within an infinite distance of the effect. Our southern view at that time, with the clouds and atmospherical hues, is quite indescribable and unimaginable; and the various distances of the hills which lie between us and the remote dome of Taconic, are brought out with an accuracy unattainable in summer. The transparency of the air at this season has the effect of a telescope in bringing objects apparently near, while it leaves the scene all its breadth. The sunset sky, amidst its splendour, has a softness and delicacy that impart themselves to a white marble world.

February 18*th*.—A walk, yesterday afternoon, with the children; a bright, and rather cold day, breezy from the north and westward. There has been a good deal of soaking rain lately, and it has, in great measure, cleared hills and plains of snow, only it may be seen lying in spots, and on each side of stone walls, in a pretty broad streak. The grass is brown and withered, and yet, scattered all amongst it, on close inspection, one finds a greenness,—little shrubs that have kept green under all the severity of winter, and seem to need no change to fit them for midsummer. In the woods we see stones covered with moss that retains likewise a most lively green. Where the trees are dense, the snow still lies under them. On the sides of the mountains, some miles off, the black pines and the white snow among them together produce a gray effect. The little streams are the most interesting objects at this time; some that have an existence only at this season,—Mississippis of the moment,— yet glide and tumble along as if they were perennial. The familiar ones seem strange by their breadth and volume; their little waterfalls set off by glaciers on a small scale. The sun has by this time force enough to make sheltered nooks in the angles of woods, or on banks, warm and comfortable. The lake is still of adamantine substance, but all round the borders there is a watery margin, altogether strewed or covered with thin and broken ice, so that I could not venture on it with the children. A chickadee was calling in the woods yesterday,—the only small bird I have taken note of yet ; but crows have been cawing in the woods for a week past, though not in very great numbers.

February 22nd.—For the last two or three days there has been a warm, soaking, south-easterly rain, with a spongy moisture diffused through the atmosphere. The snow has disappeared, except in spots which are the ruins of high drifts, and patches far up on the hillsides. The mists rest all day long on the brows of the hills that shut in our valley. The road over which I walk every day to and from the village is in the worst state of mud and mire, soft, slippery, nasty to tread upon ; while the grass beside it is scarcely better, being so oozy and so overflowed with little streams, and sometimes an absolute bog. The rivulets race along the road, adown the hills ; and wherever there is a permanent brooklet, however generally insignificant, it is now swollen into importance, and the rumble and tumble of its waterfalls may be heard a long way off. The general effect of the day and scenery is black, black, black. The streams are all as turbid as mud-puddles.

Imitators of original authors might be compared to plaster casts of marble statues, or the imitative book to a cast of the original marble.

March 11*th.*—After the ground had been completely freed of snow, there has been a snow-storm for the two days preceding yesterday, which made the earth all white again. This morning, at sunrise, the thermometer stood at about 18° above zero. Monument Mountain stands out in great prominence, with its dark forest-covered sides, and here and there a large, white patch, indicating tillage or pasture land; but making a generally dark contrast with the white expanse of the frozen and snow-covered lake at its base, and the more undulating white of the surrounding country. Yesterday, under the sunshine of midday, and with many voluminous clouds hanging over it, and a mist of wintry warmth in the air, it had a kind of visionary aspect, although still it was brought out in striking relief. But though one could see all its bulgings, round swells, and precipitous abruptnesses, it looked as much akin to the clouds as to solid earth and rock substance. In the early sunshine of the morning, the atmosphere being very clear, I saw the dome of Taconic with more distinctness than ever before, the snow-patches and brown uncovered soil on its round head being fully visible. Generally it is but a dark blue unvaried mountain-top. All the ruggedness of the intervening hill-country was likewise effectively brought out. There seems to be a sort of illuminating quality in new snow, which it loses after being exposed for a day or two to the sun and atmosphere.

For a child's story,—the voyage of a little boat, made of a chip, with a birch-bark sail, down a river.

March 31*st.*—A walk with the children yesterday forenoon. We went through the wood, where we found partridge-berries, half hidden among the dry, fallen leaves; thence down to the brook. This little brook has not cleansed itself from the disarray of the past autumn and winter, and is much embarrassed and choked up with brown leaves, twigs, and bits of branches. It rushes along merrily and rapidly, gurgling cheerfully, and tumbling over the impediments of stones with which the children and I made little waterfalls last year. At many spots there are small basins or pools of calmer and smoother depth,

—three feet, perhaps, in diameter, and a foot or two deep,—in which little fish are already sporting about; all elsewhere is tumble and gurgle and mimic turbulence. I sat on the withered leaves at the foot of a tree, while the children played, a little brook being the most fascinating plaything that a child can have. Una jumped to and fro across it; Julian stood beside a pool, fishing with a stick, without hook or line, and wondering that he caught nothing. Then he made new waterfalls with mighty labour, pulling big stones out of the earth, and flinging them into the current. Then they sent branches of trees, or the outer shells of walnuts, sailing down the stream, and watched their passages through the intricacies of the way,—how they were hurried over in a cascade, hurried dizzily round in a whirlpool, or brought quite to a stand-still amongst the collected rubbish. At last Julian tumbled into the brook, and was wetted through and through, so that we were obliged to come home; he squelching along all the way, with his india-rubber shoes full of water.

There are still patches of snow on the hills; also in the woods, especially on the northern margins. The lake is not yet what we may call thawed out, although there is a large space of blue water, and the ice is separated from the shore everywhere, and is soft, water-soaked, and crumbly. On favourable slopes and exposures the earth begins to look green; and almost anywhere, if one looks closely, one sees the greenness of the grass, or of little herbage, amidst the brown. Under the nut-trees are scattered some of the nuts of last year; the walnuts have lost their virtue, the chestnuts do not seem to have much taste, but the butternuts are in no manner deteriorated. The warmth of these days has a mistiness, and in many respects resembles the Indian summer, and is not at all provocative of physical exertion. Nevertheless, the general impression is of life, not death. One feels that a new season has begun.

Wednesday, April 9th.—There was a great rain yesterday,—wind from the south-east, and the last visible vestige of snow disappeared. It was a small patch near the summit of Bald Mountain, just on the upper verge of a grove of trees. I saw a slight remnant of it yesterday afternoon, but to-day it is quite gone. The grass comes up along the roadside and on favourable exposures, with a sort of green blush. Frogs have been melodious for a fortnight, and the birds sing pleasantly.

April 20*th*. — The children found Houstonias more than a week ago. There have been easterly wind, continual cloudiness, and occasional rain for a week. This morning opened with a great snow-storm from the north-east, one of the most earnest snow-storms of the year, though rather more moist than [in midwinter. The earth is entirely covered. Now, as the day advances towards noon, it shows some symptoms of turning to rain.

April 28*th*.—For a week we have found the trailing arbutus pretty abundant in the woods. A day or two since, Una found a few purple violets, and yesterday a dandelion in bloom. The fragrance of the arbutus is spicy and exquisite.

May 16*th*.—In our walks now, the children and I find blue, white, and golden violets, the former, especially, of great size and richness. Houstonias are very abundant, blue-whitening some of the pastures. They are a very sociable little flower, and dwell close together in communities,—sometimes covering a space no larger than the palm of the hand, but keeping one another in cheerful heart and life,— sometimes they occupy a much larger space. Lobelia, a pink flower, growing in the woods. Columbines, of a pale red, because they have lacked sun, growing in rough and rocky places on banks in the copses, precipitating towards the lake. The leaves of the trees are not yet out, but are so apparent that the woods are getting a very decided shadow. Water-weeds on the edge of the lake, of a deep green, with roots that seem to have nothing to do with earth, but with water only.

May 23rd.—I think the face of nature can never look more beautiful than now, with this so fresh and youthful green,—the trees not being fully in leaf, yet enough so to give airy shade to the woods. The sunshine fills them with green light. Monument Mountain and its brethren are green, and the lightness of the tint takes away something from their massiveness and ponderosity, and they respond with livelier effect to the shine and shade of the sky. Each tree now within sight stands out in its own individuality of hue. This is a very windy day, and the light shifts with magical alternation. In a walk to the lake just now with the children, we found abundance of flowers,—wild geranium, violets of all families, red columbines, and many others known and unknown, besides innumerable blossoms of the wild strawberry, which has been in bloom for the past fortnight. The Houstonias seem quite to overspread some pastures, when viewed from a distance. Not merely the flowers, but the various shrubs which one sees,—seated, for instance, on the decayed trunk of a tree,—are well worth looking at, such a variety and such enjoyment they have of their new growth. Amid these fresh creations, we see others that have already run their course, and have done with warmth and sunshine,—the hoary periwigs, I mean, of dandelions gone to seed.

August 7th.—Fourier states that, in the progress of the world, the ocean is to lose its saltness, and acquire the taste of a peculiarly flavoured lemonade.

October 13th.—How pleasant it is to see a human countenance which cannot be insincere,—in reference to baby's smile.

The best of us being unfit to die, what an inexpressible absurdity to put the worst to death!

" Is that a burden of sunshine on Apollo's back ? "

asked one of the children,—of the chlamys on our Apollo Belvedere.

October 21*st.*—Going to the village yesterday afternoon, I saw the face of a beautiful woman, gazing at me from a cloud. It was the full face, not the bust. It had a sort of mantle on the head, and a pleasant expression of countenance. The vision lasted while I took a few steps, and then vanished. I never before saw nearly so distinct a cloud-picture, or rather sculpture; for it came out in alto-relievo on the body of the cloud.

October 27*th.*—The ground this morning is white with a thin covering of snow. The foliage has still some variety of hue. The dome of Taconic looks dark, and seems to have no snow on it, though I don't understand how that can be. I saw, a moment ago, on the lake, a very singular spectacle. There is a high north-west wind ruffling the lake's surface, and making it blue, lead-coloured, or bright, in stripes or at intervals; but what I saw was a boiling up of foam, which began at the right bank of the lake, and passed quite across it; and the mist flew before it, like the cloud out of a steam-engine. A fierce and narrow blast of wind must have ploughed the water in a straight line, from side to side of the lake. As fast as it went on, the foam subsided behind it, so that it looked somewhat like a sea-serpent, or other monster, swimming very rapidly.

October 29th.—On a walk to Scott's pond, with Ellery Channing, we found a wild strawberry in the woods, not quite ripe, but beginning to redden. For a week or two, the cider-mills have been grinding apples. Immense heaps of apples lie piled near them, and the creaking of the press is heard as the horse treads on. Farmers are repairing cider-barrels; and the wayside brook is made to pour itself into the bunghole of a barrel, in order to cleanse it for the new cider.

November 3rd.—The face of the country is dreary now in a cloudy day like the present. The woods on the hillsides look almost black, and the cleared spaces a kind of grey brown.

Taconic, this morning (4th) was a black purple, as dense and distinct as Monument Mountain itself. I hear the creaking of the cider-press; the patient horse going round and round, perhaps thirsty, to make the liquor which he never can enjoy.

We left Lenox Friday morning, November 21, 1851, in a storm of snow and sleet, and took the cars at Pittsfield, and arrived at West Newton that evening.

Happiness in this world, when it comes, comes incidentally. Make it the object of pursuit, and it leads us a wild-goose chase, and is never attained. Follow some other object, and very possibly we may find that we have caught happiness, without dreaming of it; but likely enough it is gone the moment we say to ourselves, "Here it is!" like the chest of gold that treasure-seekers find.

West Newton, April 13*th*, 1852. — One of the severest snow-storms of the winter.

April 30*th.*—Wrote the last page (199th MS.) of the *Blithedale Romance.*

May 1*st.*—Wrote Preface. Afterwards modified the conclusion, and lengthened it to 201 pages. First proof-sheets, May 14.

Concord, Mass., August 20*th.*—A piece of land

contiguous to and connected with a handsome estate, to the adornment and good appearance of which it was essential. But the owner of the strip of land was at variance with the owner of the estate, so he always refused to sell it at any price, but let it lie there, wild and ragged, in front of and near the mansion-house. When he dies, the owner of the estate, who has rejoiced at the approach of the event all through his enemy's illness, hopes at last to buy it; but, to his infinite discomfiture, the enemy enjoined in his will that his body should be buried in the centre of this strip of land. All sorts of ugly weeds grow most luxuriantly out of the grave in poisonous rankness.

The Isles of Shoals, Monday, August 30*th*.—Left Concord at a quarter of nine, A.M. Friday, September 3, set sail at about half-past ten to the Isles of Shoals. The passengers were an old master of a vessel; a young, rather genteel man from Greenland, N. H.; two Yankees from Hamilton and Danvers; and a country trader (I should judge) from some inland town of New Hampshire. The old sea-captain, preparatory to sailing, bought a bunch of cigars (they cost ten cents), and occasionally puffed one. The two Yankees had brought guns on board, and asked questions about the fishing of the Shoals. They were young men, brothers, the youngest a shopkeeper in Danvers, the other a farmer, I imagine, at Hamilton, and both specimens of the least polished kind of Yankee, and therefore proper to those localities. They were at first full of questions, and greatly interested in whatever was going forward; but anon the shopkeeper began to grow, first a little, then very sick, till he lay along the boat, longing, as he afterwards said, for a little fresh water to be drowned in. His brother attended him in a very kindly way, but became sick himself before he reached the end of the voyage.

The young Greenlander talked politics, or rather, discussed the personal character of Pierce. The New Hampshire trader said not a word, or hardly one, all the way. A Portsmouth youth (whom I forgot to mention) sat in the stern of the boat, looking very white. The skipper of the boat is a Norwegian, a good-natured fellow, not particularly intelligent, and speaking in a dialect somewhat like Irish. He had a man with him, a silent and rather sulky fellow, who, at the captain's bidding, grimly made himself useful.

The wind not being favourable, we had to make

several tacks before reaching the islands, where we arrived at about two o'clock. We landed at Appledore, on which is Laighton's Hotel,—a large building with a piazza or promenade before it, about an hundred and twenty feet in length, or more,—yes, it must be more. It is an edifice with a centre and two wings, the central part upwards of seventy feet. At one end of the promenade is a covered verandah, thirty or forty feet square, so situated that the breeze draws across it from the sea on one side of the island to the sea on the other, and it is the breeziest and comfortablest place in the world on a hot day. There are two swings beneath it, and here one may sit or walk, and enjoy life, while all other mortals are suffering.

As I entered the door of the hotel, there met me a short, corpulent, round, and full-faced man, rather elderly, if not old. He was a little lame. He addressed me in a hearty, hospitable tone, and, judging that it must be my landlord, I delivered a letter of introduction from Pierce. Of course it was fully efficient in obtaining the best accommodations that were to be had. I found that we were expected, a man having brought the news of our intention the day before. Here ensued great inquiries after the General, and wherefore he had not come. I was looked at with considerable curiosity on my own account, especially by the ladies, of whom there were several, agreeable and pretty enough. There were four or five gentlemen, most of whom had not much that was noteworthy.

After dinner, which was good and abundant, though somewhat rude in its style, I was introduced by Mr. Laighton to Mr. Thaxter, his son-in-law, and Mr. Weiss, a clergyman of New Bedford, who is staying here for his health. They showed me some of the remarkable features of the island, such as a deep chasm in the cliffs of the shore, towards the south-west; also a monument of rude stones, on the highest point of the island, said to have been erected by Captain John Smith before the settlement at Plymouth. The tradition is just as good as truth. Also, some ancient cellars, with thistles and other weeds growing in them, and old fragmentary bricks scattered about. The date of these habitations is not known; but they may well be the remains of the settlement that Cotton Mather speaks about; or perhaps one of them was the house where Sir William Pepperell was born, and where he went when he and somebody else set up a stick, and travelled to seek their fortunes in the direction in which it fell.

In the evening, the company at the hotel made up two whist-parties, at one of which I sat down,—my partner being an agreeable young lady from Portsmouth. We played till I, at least, was quite weary. It had been the beautifullest of weather all day, very hot on the mainland, but a delicious climate under our verandah.

Saturday, September 4th.—Another beautiful day, rather cooler than the preceding, but not too cool. I can bear this coolness better than that of the interior. In the forenoon, I took passage for Star Island, in a boat that crosses daily whenever there are passengers. My companions were the two Yankees, who had quite recovered from yesterday's sickness, and were in the best of spirits and the utmost activity of mind of which they were capable. Never was there such a string of questions as they directed to the boatman,—questions that seemed to have no gist, so far as related to any use that could be made of the answers. They appear to be very good young men, however, well-meaning, and with manners not disagreeable, because their hearts are not amiss. Star Island is less than a mile from Appledore. It is the most populous island of the group,—has been, for three or four years, an incorporated township, and sends a representative to the New Hampshire legislature. The number of voters is variously represented as from eighteen to twenty-eight. The inhabitants are all, I presume, fishermen. Their houses stand in pretty close neighbourhood to one another, scattered about without the slightest regularity or pretence of a street, there being no wheel-carriages on the island. Some of the houses are very comfortable two-storey dwellings. I saw two or three, I think, with flowers. There are also one or two trees on the island. There is a strong odour of fishiness, and the little cove is full of mackerel-boats, and other small craft for fishing, in some of which little boys of no growth at all were paddling about. Nearly in the centre of this insular metropolis is a two-storey house, with a flag-staff in the yard. This is the hotel.

On the highest point of Star Island stands the church,—a small, wooden structure; and, sitting in its shadow, I found a red-baize-shirted fisherman, who seemed quite willing to converse. He said that there was a minister here, who was also the schoolmaster; but that he did not keep school just now, because his wife was very much out of health. The school-house stood but a little way from the meeting-house, and near it was the minister's dwelling; and by and by I had a glimpse of the good man himself, in his suit of black, which looked in very decent condition at the distance from which I viewed it. His clerical air was quite distinguishable, and it was rather curious to see it, when everybody else wore red-baize shirts and fishing-boots, and looked of the scaly genus. He did not approach me, and I saw him no nearer. I soon grew weary of Gosport, and was glad to re-embark, although I intend to revisit the island with Mr. Thaxter, and see more of its peculiarities and inhabitants. I saw one old witch-looking woman creeping about with a cane, and stooping down, seemingly to gather herbs. On mentioning her to Mr. Thaxter, after my return, he said that it was probably "the bearded woman." I did not observe her beard; but very likely she may have had one.

The larger part of the company at the hotel returned to the mainland to-day. There remained behind, however, a Mr. T—— from Newburyport,—a man of natural refinement, and a taste for reading that seems to point towards the writings of Emerson, Thoreau, and men of that class. I have had a good deal of talk with him, and at first doubted whether he might not be a clergyman; but Mr. Thaxter tells me that he has made his own way in the world,—was once a sailor before the mast, and is now engaged in mercantile pursuits. He looks like nothing of this kind, being tall and slender, with very quiet manners, not beautiful, though pleasing from the refinement that they indicate. He has rather a precise and careful pronunciation, but yet a natural way of talking.

* * * * *

In the afternoon I walked round a portion of the island that I had not previously visited, and in the evening went with Mr. Titcomb to Mr. Thaxter's to drink apple-toddy. We found Mrs. Thaxter sitting in a neat little parlour, very simply furnished, but in good taste. She is not now, I believe, more than eighteen years old, very pretty, and with the manners of a lady,—not prim and precise, but with enough of freedom and ease. The books on the table were "Pre-Raphaelitism," a tract on spiritual mediums, &c. There were several shelves of books on one side of the room, and engravings on the walls. Mr. Weiss was there, and I do not know but he is an inmate of Mr. Thaxter's. By and by came in Mr. Thaxter's brother, with a young lady, whose position I do not know,—either a sister or the brother's wife. Anon, too, came in the apple-toddy, a very rich and spicy compound; after which we had some glees and negro melodies, in which Mr. Thaxter sang a noble bass, and Mrs. Thaxter sang like a bird, and Mr. Weiss sang, I suppose, tenor, and the brother took some other part, and all were very mirthful and jolly. At about ten o'clock Mr. Titcomb and myself took leave, and emerging into the open air, out of that room of song, and pretty youthfulness of woman, and gay young men, there was the sky, and the three-quarters waning moon, and the old sea moaning all round about the island.

Sunday, September 5th.—To-day I have done little or nothing except to roam along the shore of the island, and to sit under the piazza, talking with Mr. Laighton or some of his half-dozen guests; and about an hour before dinner I came up to my room, and took a brief nap. Since dinner I have been writing the foregoing journal. I observe that the "Fanny Ellsler," our passenger and mail boat, has arrived from Portsmouth, and now lies in a little cove, moored to the rocky shore, with a flag flying at her mainmast. We have been watching her for some hours, but she stopped to fish, and then went to some other island, before putting in here. I must go and see what news she has brought.

"What did you fire at?" asked one of the Yankees just now of a boy who had been firing a gun. "Nothing," said the boy. "Did you hit it?" rejoined the Yankee.

The farmer is of a much ruder and rougher mould than his brother,—heavier in frame and mind, and far less cultivated. It was on this account, probably, that he laboured as a farmer, instead of setting up a shop. When it is warm, as yesterday, he takes off his coat, and, not minding whether or no his shirt-sleeves be soiled, goes in this guise to meals or wherever else, —not resuming his coat as long as he is more comfortable without it. His shoulders have a stoop, and altogether his air is that of a farmer in repose. His brother is handsome and might have quite the aspect of a smart, comely young man, if well dressed.

This island is said to be haunted by a spectre called "Old Bab." He was one of Captain Kidd's men, and was slain for the protection of the treasure. Mr. Laighton said that, before he built his house, nothing would have induced the inhabitant of another island to come to this after nightfall. The ghost especially haunts the space between the hotel and the cove in front. There has, in times past, been great search for the treasure.

Mr. Thaxter tells me that the women on the island are very timid as to venturing on the sea,— more so than the women of the mainland,—and that they are easily frightened about their husbands. Very few accidents happen to the boats or men,— none, I think, since Mr. Thaxter has been here. They are not an enterprising set of people, never liking to make long voyages. Sometimes one of them will ship on a voyage to the West Indies, but generally only on coastwise trips, or fishing or mackerel voyages. They have a very strong local attachment, and return to die. They are now generally temperate, formerly very much the contrary.

September 6th.—A large part of the guests took their departure after an early breakfast this morning, including Mr. Titcomb, Mr. Weiss, the two Yankees, and Mr. Thaxter,—who, however, went as skipper or supercargo, and will return with the boat. I have been fishing for cunners off the rocks, but with intolerably poor success. There is nothing so dispiriting as poor fishing, and I spend most of the time with my head on my hands, looking at the sea breaking against the rocks, shagged around the bases with seaweed. It is a sunny forenoon, with a cool breeze from the south-west. The mackerel craft are in the offing. Mr. Laighton says that the "Spy" (the boat which went to the mainland this morning) is now on her return with all her colours set; and he thinks that Pierce is on board, he having sent Mr. Thaxter to invite him to come in this boat.

Pierce arrived before dinner in the "Spy," accompanied by Judge Upham and his brother and their wives, his own wife, Mr. Furness, and three young ladies. After dinner some of the gentlemen crossed over to Gosport, where we visited the old graveyard, in which were monuments to Rev. Mr. Tucke (died 1773, after forty years' settlement) and to another and later minister of the island. They were of red freestone, lying horizontally on piles of the granite fragments, such as are scattered all about. There were other graves, marked by the rudest shapes of stones at head and foot. And so many stones protruded from the ground, that it was wonderful how space and depth enough was found between them to cover the dead. We went to the house of the town clerk of Gosport, (a drunken fisherman, Joe Caswell by name,) and there found the town records, commencing in 1732, in a beautiful style of penmanship. They are imperfect, the township having been broken up, probably at the time of the Revolution. Caswell, being very drunk, immediately put in a petition to Pierce to build a sea-mole for the protection of the navigation of the island, when he should be President. He was dressed in the ordinary fisherman's style,— red-baize shirt, trousers tucked into large boots, which, as he had just come ashore, were wet with salt water.

He led us down to the shore of the island, towards the east, and showed us Betty Moody's Hole. This Betty Moody was a woman of the island in old times. The Indians came off on a depredating excursion, and she fled from them with a child, and hid herself in this hole, which is formed by several great rocks being lodged so as to cover one of the fissures which are common along these shores. I crept into the hole, which is somewhat difficult of access, long, low, and narrow, and might well enough be a hiding-place. The child, or children, began to cry; and Betty, fearful of discovery, murdered them to save herself. Joe Caswell did not tell the latter part of the story, but Mr. Thaxter did.

Not far from the spot there is a point of rocks extending out farther into the ocean than the rest of the island. Some four or five years ago there was a young woman residing at Gosport in the capacity of school-teacher. She was of a romantic turn, and used to go and sit on this point of rock to view the waves. One day, when the wind was high, and the surf raging against the rocks, a great wave struck her, as she sat on the edge, and seemed to deprive her of sense; another wave, or the reflex of the same one, carried her off into the sea, and she was seen no more. This happened, I think, in 1846.

Passing a rock near the centre of the island, which rose from the soil about breast-high, and appeared to have been split asunder, with an incalculably aged and moss-grown fissure, the surfaces of which, however, precisely suited each other, Mr. Hatch mentioned that there was an idea among the people, with regard to rocks thus split, that they were rent asunder at the time of the Crucifixion. Judge Upham observed that this superstition was common in all parts of the country.

Mr. Hatch said that he was professionally consulted, the other day, by a man who had been digging for buried treasure at Dover Point, up the Piscataqua River; and, while he and his companions were thus engaged, the owner of the land came upon them, and compelled Hatch's client to give him a note for a sum of money. The object was to inquire whether this note was obligatory. Hatch says that there are a hundred people now resident in Portsmouth, who, at one time or another, have dug for treasure. The process is, in the first place, to find out the site of the treasure by the divining-rod. A circle is then described with the steel rod about the spot, and a man walks around within its verge, reading the Bible to keep off the evil spirit while his companions dig. If a word is spoken, the whole business is a failure. Once the person who told him the story reached the lid of the chest, so that the spades plainly scraped upon it, when one of the men spoke, and the chest immediately moved sideways into the earth. Another time, when he was reading the Bible within the circle, a creature like a white horse, but immoderately large, came from a distance towards the circle, looked at him, and then began to graze about the spot. He saw the motion of the jaws, but heard no sound of champing. His companions saw the gigantic horse precisely as he did, only to them it appeared bay instead of white.

The islanders stared with great curiosity at Pierce. One pretty young woman appeared inclined to engross him entirely to herself.

There is a bowling-alley on the island, at which some of the young fishermen were rolling.

September 7th.— . . . I have made no exploration to-day, except a walk with the guests in the morning, but have lounged about the piazza and verandah. It has been a calm, warm, sunny day, the sea slumbering against the shores, and now and then breaking into white foam.

The surface of the island is plentifully overgrown with whortleberry and bayberry bushes. The sheep cut down the former, so that few berries are produced; the latter gives a pleasant fragrance when pressed in the hand. The island is one great ledge of rock, four hundred acres in extent, with a little soil thrown scantily over it; but the bare rock everywhere emerging, not only in points, but still more in flat surfaces. The only trees, I think, are two that Mr. Laighton has been trying to raise in front of the hotel, the taller of which looks scarcely so much as ten feet high. It is now about sunset, and the "Fanny," with the mail, is just arrived at the moorings. So still is it, that the sounds on board (as of throwing oars into a small boat) are distinctly heard, though a quarter of a mile off. She has the Stars and

Stripes flying at the mainmast. There appear to be no passengers.

The only reptile on the island is a very vivid and beautiful green snake, which is exceedingly abundant. Yesterday, while catching grasshoppers for fish-bait, I nearly griped one in my hand; indeed, I rather think I did gripe it. The snake was as much startled as myself, and, in its fright, stood an instant on its tail, before it recovered presence of mind to glide away. These snakes are quite harmless.

September 8th.—Last evening we could hear the roaring of the beaches at Hampton and Rye, nine miles off. The surf likewise swelled against the rocky shores of the island, though there was little or no wind, and, except for the swell, the surface was smooth. The sheep bleated loudly; and all these tokens, according to Mr. Laighton, foreboded a storm to windward. This morning, nevertheless, there were no further signs of it; it is sunny and calm, or only the slightest breeze from the westward; a haze sleeping along the shore, betokening a warm day; the surface of the sea streaked with smoothness, and gentle ruffles of wind. It has been the hottest day that I have known here, and probably one of the hottest of the season ashore; and the land is now imperceptible in the haze.

Smith's monument is about seven feet high, and probably ten or twelve in diameter at its base. It is a cairn, or mere heap of stones, thrown together as they came to hand, though with some selection of large and flat ones towards the base, and with smaller ones thrown in. At the foundation there are large rocks, naturally embedded in the earth. I see no reason to disbelieve that a part of this monument may have been erected by Captain Smith, although subsequent visitors may have added to it. Laighton says it is known to have stood upwards of a hundred years. It is a work of considerable labour, and would more likely have been erected by one who supposed himself the first discoverer of the island than by anybody afterwards for mere amusement. I observed in some places, towards the base, that the lichens had grown from one stone to another; and there is nothing in the appearance of the monument that controverts the supposition of its antiquity. It is an irregular circle, somewhat decreasing towards the top. Few of the stones, except at the base, are bigger than a man could easily lift,—many of them are not more than a foot across. It stands towards the southern part of the island; and all the other islands are visible from it,—Smutty Nose, Star Island, and White Island,—on which is the light-house,—much of Laighton's island (the proper name of which is Hog, though latterly called Appledore), and Duck Island, which looks like a mere reef of rocks, and about a mile farther into the ocean, easterly of Hog Island.

Laighton's Hotel, together with the house in which his son-in-law resides, which was likewise built by Laighton, and stands about fifty yards from the hotel, occupies the middle of a shallow valley, which passes through the island from east to west. Looking from the verandah, you have the ocean opening towards the east, and the bay towards Rye Beach and Portsmouth on the west. In the same storm that overthrew Minot's Light, a year or two ago, a great wave passed entirely through this valley; and Laighton describes it, when it came in from the sea, as toppling over to the height of the cupola of his hotel. It roared and whitened through, from sea to sea, twenty feet abreast, rolling along huge rocks in its passage. It passed beneath his verandah, which stands on posts, and probably filled the valley completely. Would I had been here to see!

The day has been exceedingly hot. Since dinner,

the "Spy" has arrived from Portsmouth, with a party of half a dozen or more men and women and children, apparently from the interior of New Hampshire. I am rather sorry to receive these strangers into the quiet life that we are leading here; for we had grown quite to feel ourselves at home, and the two young ladies, Mr. Thaxter, his wife and sister, and myself, met at meal-times like one family. The young ladies gathered shells, arranged them, laughed gently, sang, and did other pretty things in a young-lady-like way. These new-comers are people of uncouth voices and loud laughter, and behave themselves as if they were trying to turn their expedition to as much account as possible in the way of enjoyment.

John's boat, the regular passenger-boat, is now coming in, and probably brings the mail.

In the afternoon, while some of the new-comers were fishing off the rocks, west of the hotel, a shark came close in shore. Hearing their outcries, I looked out of my chamber window, and saw the dorsal fin and the fluke of his tail stuck up out of the water, as he moved to and fro. He must have been eight or ten feet long. He had probably followed the small fish into the bay, and got bewildered, and, at one time, he was almost aground.

Oscar, Mr. Laighton's son, ran down with a gun, and fired at the shark, which was then not more than ten yards from the shore. He aimed, according to his father's directions, just below the junction of the dorsal fin with the body; but the gun was loaded only with shot, and seemed to produce no effect. Oscar had another shot at him afterwards; the shark floundered a little in the water, but finally got off and disappeared, probably without very serious damage. He came so near the shore that he might have been touched with a boat-hook.

September 9th.—Mr. Thaxter rowed me this morning, in his dory, to White Island, on which is the lighthouse. There was scarcely a breath of air, and a perfectly calm sea; an intensely hot sunshine, with a little haze, so that the horizon was indistinct. Here and there sail-boats sleeping on the water, or moving almost imperceptibly over it. The lighthouse island would be difficult of access in a rough sea, the shore being so rocky. On landing, we found the keeper peeling his harvest of onions, which he had gathered prematurely, because the insects were eating them. His little patch of garden seemed to be a strange kind of soil, as like marine mud as anything; but he had a fair crop of marrow squashes, though injured, as he said, by the last storm; and there were cabbages and a few turnips. I recollect no other garden vegetables. The grass grows pretty luxuriantly, and looked very green where there was any soil; but he kept no cow, nor even a pig nor a hen. His house stands close by the garden,—a small stone building, with peaked roof, and whitewashed. The lighthouse stands on a ledge of rock, with a gulley between, and there is a long covered way, triangular in shape, connecting his residence with it. We ascended into the lantern, which is eighty-seven feet high. It is a revolving light, with several great illuminators of copper silvered, and coloured lamp-glasses. Looking downwards, we had the island displayed as on a chart, with its little bays, its isthmus of shingly beach connecting two parts of the island, and overflowed at high tide; its sunken rocks about it, indicated by the swell, or slightly breaking surf. The keeper of the lighthouse was formerly a writing-master. He has a sneaking kind of look, and does not bear a very high character among his neighbours. Since he kept the light, he has lost two wives,—the first a young creature whom he used to leave alone upon this desolate rock, and the gloom and terror of the situation were probably the cause of her death. The second wife, experiencing the same kind of treatment, ran away from him, and returned to her friends. He pretends to be religious, but drinks. About a year ago he attempted to row out alone from Portsmouth. There was a head wind and head tide, and he would have inevitably drifted out to sea, if Mr. Thaxter had not saved him.

While we were standing in his garden-patch, I heard a woman's voice inside the dwelling, but know not whose it was. A lighthouse nine miles from shore would be a delightful place for a new-married couple to spend their honeymoon, or their whole first year.

On our way back we landed at another island called Londoner's Rock, or some such name. It has but little soil. As we approached it, a large bird flew away. Mr. Thaxter took it to be a gannet; and, while walking over the island, an owl started up from among the rocks near us, and flew away, apparently uncertain of its course. It was a brown owl, but Mr. Thaxter says that there are beautiful white owls, which spend the winter here, and feed upon rats. These are very abundant, and live amidst the rocks,—probably having been brought hither by vessels.

The water to-day was not so transparent as sometimes, but had a slight haze diffused through it, somewhat like that of the atmosphere.

The passengers brought by the "Spy," yesterday, still remain with us. They consist of country traders, a country doctor, and such sorts of people, rude, shrewd, and simple, and well-behaved enough; wondering at sharks, and equally at lobsters; sitting down to table with their coats off; helping themselves out of the dish with their own forks; taking pudding on the plates off which they have eaten meat. People at just this stage of manners are more disagreeable than at any other stage. They are aware of some decencies, but not so deeply aware as to make them a matter of conscience. They may be heard talking of the financial affairs of the expedition, reckoning what money each has paid. One offers to pay another three or four cents, which the latter has overpaid. "It's of no consequence, sir," says his friend, with a tone of conscious liberality, "that's near enough." This is a most tremendously hot day.

There is a young lady staying at the hotel, afflicted

with what her friends call erysipelas, but which is probably scrofula. She seems unable to walk, or sit up; but every pleasant day, about the middle of the forenoon, she is dragged out beneath the verandah, on a sofa. To-day she has been there until late in the decline of the afternoon. It is a delightful place, where the breezes stir, if any are in motion. The young girls, her sisters or cousins, and Mr. Thaxter's sister, sat round her, babbling cheerfully, and singing; and they were so merry that it did not seem as if there could be an incurably sick one in the midst of them.

The "Spy" came to-day, with more passengers of no particular character. She still remains off the landing, moored, with her sails in the wind.

The mail arrived to-day, but nothing for me.

Close by the verandah, at the end of the hotel, is drawn up a large boat, of ten or twelve tons, which got injured in some gale, and probably will remain there for years to decay, and be a picturesque and characteristic object.

The "Spy" has been lying in the broad track of golden light, thrown by the sun, far down towards the horizon, over the rippling water, her sails throwing distinct, dark shadows over the brightness. She has now got under way, and set sail on a north-west course for Portsmouth; carrying off, I believe, all the passengers she brought to-day.

September 10th.—Here is another beautiful morning, with the sun dimpling in the early sunshine. Four sail-boats are in sight, motionless on the sea, with the whiteness of their sails reflected in it. The heat-haze sleeps along the shore, though not so as quite to hide it, and there is the promise of another very warm day. As yet, however, the air is cool and refreshing. Around the island there is the little ruffle of a breeze; but where the sail-boats are, a mile or more off, the sea is perfectly calm. The crickets sing, and I hear the chirping of birds besides.

At the base of the lighthouse yesterday, we saw the wings and feathers of a decayed little bird, and Mr. Thaxter said they often flew against the lantern with such force as to kill themselves, and that large quantities of them might be picked up. How came these little birds out of their nests at night? Why should they meet destruction from the radiance that proves the salvation of other beings?

Mr. Thaxter had once a man living with him who had seen "Old Bab," the ghost. He met him between the hotel and the sea, and describes him as dressed in a sort of frock, and with a very dreadful countenance.

Two or three years ago, the crew of a wrecked vessel, a brigantine, wrecked near Boon Island, landed on Hog Island of a winter night, and found shelter in the hotel. It was from the eastward. There were six or seven men, with the mate and captain. It was midnight when they got ashore. The common sailors, as soon as they were physically comfortable, seemed to be perfectly at ease. The captain walked the floor, bemoaning himself for a silver watch which he had lost; the mate, being the only married man, talked about his Eunice. They all told their dreams of the preceding night, and saw in them prognostics of the misfortune.

There is now a breeze, the blue ruffle of which seems to reach almost across to the mainland, yet with streaks of calm; and, in one place, the glassy surface of a lake of calmness, amidst the surrounding commotion.

The wind, in the early morning, was from the west, and the aspect of the sky seemed to promise a warm and sunny day. But all at once, soon after breakfast, the wind shifted round to the eastward; and great volumes of fog, almost as dense as cannon-smoke, came sweeping from the eastern ocean, through the valley, and past the house. It soon covered the whole sea, and the whole island, beyond a verge of a few hundred yards. The chilliness was not so great as accompanies a change of wind on the mainland. We had been watching a large ship that was slowly making her way between us and the land towards Portsmouth. This was now hidden. The breeze is still very moderate; but the boat, moored near the shore, rides with a considerable motion, as if the sea were getting up.

Mr. Laighton says that the artist who adorned Trinity Church in New York with sculpture wanted some real wings from which to imitate the wings of cherubim. Mr. Thaxter carried him the wings of the white owl that winters here at the Shoals, together with those of some other bird; and the artist gave his cherubim the wings of an owl.

This morning there have been two boat-loads of visitors from Rye. They merely made a flying call, and took to their boats again,— a disagreeable and impertinent kind of people.

The "Spy" arrived before dinner, with several passengers. After dinner came the "Fanny," bringing, among other freight, a large basket of delicious pears to me, together with a note from Mr. B. B. Titcomb. He is certainly a man of excellent taste and admirable behaviour. I sent a plateful of pears to the room of each guest now in the hotel, kept a dozen for myself, and gave the balance to Mr. Laighton.

The two Portsmouth young ladies returned in the "Spy." I had grown accustomed to their presence, and rather liked them; one of them being gay and rather noisy, and the other quiet and gentle. As to new-comers, I feel rather a distaste to them; and so, I find, does Mr. Laighton,—a rather singular sentiment for a hotel-keeper to entertain towards his guests. However, he treats them very hospitably, when once within his doors.

The sky is overcast, and, about the time the "Spy" and the "Fanny" sailed, there were a few drops of rain. The wind, at that time, was strong enough to raise white caps to the eastward of the island, and there was good hope of a storm. Now, however, the wind has subsided, and the weather-seers know not what to forebode.

September 11*th.*—The wind shifted and veered about, towards the close of yesterday, and later it was almost calm, after blowing gently from the northwest,—notwithstanding which it rained. There being a mistiness in the air, we could see the gleam of the lighthouse upon the mist above it, although the lighthouse itself was hidden by the highest point of this island, or by our being in a valley. As we sat under the piazza in the evening, we saw the light from on board some vessel move slowly through the distant obscurity,—so slowly that we were only sensible of its progress by forgetting it and looking again. The plash and murmur of the waves around the island were soothingly audible. It was not unpleasantly cold, and Mr. Laighton, Mr. Thaxter, and myself sat under the piazza till long after dark; the former at a little distance, occasionally smoking his pipe, and Mr. Thaxter and I talking about poets and the stage. The latter is an odd subject to be discussed in this stern and wild scene, which has precisely the same characteristics now as two hundred years ago. The mosquitoes were very abundant last night, and they are certainly a hardier race than their inland brethren.

This morning there is a sullen sky, with scarcely any breeze. The clouds throw shadows of varied darkness upon the sea. I know not which way the wind is; but the aspect of things seems to portend a calm drizzle as much as anything else.

About eleven o'clock Mr. Thaxter took me over to Smutty Nose in his dory. A sloop from the eastward, laden with laths, bark, and other lumber, and a few barrels of mackerel, filled yesterday, and was left by her skipper and crew. All the morning we have seen boats picking up her deck-load, which was scattered over the sea, and along the shores of the islands. The skipper and his three men got into Smutty Nose in the boat; and the sloop was afterwards boarded by the Smutty Noses, and brought into that island. We saw her lying at the pier,—a black, ugly, rotten old thing, with the water half-way over her decks. The wonder was how she swam so long. The skipper, a man of about thirty-five or forty, in a blue pilot-cloth overcoat, and a rusty, high-crowned hat jammed down over his brow, looked very forlorn; while the islanders were grouped about, indolently enjoying the matter.

I walked with Mr. Thaxter over the island, and saw first the graves of the Spaniards. They were wrecked on this island a hundred years ago, and lie buried in a range about thirty feet in length, to the number of sixteen, with rough, moss-grown pieces of granite on each side of this common grave. Near this spot, yet somewhat removed, so as not to be confounded with it, are other individual graves, chiefly of the Haley family, who were once possessors of the island. These have slate gravestones. There is also, within a small enclosure of rough pine boards, a white marble gravestone, in memory of a young man named Bekker, son of the person who now keeps the hotel on Smutty Nose. He was buried, Mr. Thaxter says, notwithstanding his marble monument, in a rude pine box, which he himself helped to make.

We walked to the farthest point of the island, and I have never seen a more dismal place than it was on this sunless and east-windy day, being the farthest point out into the melancholy sea, which was in no very agreeable mood, and roared sullenly against the wilderness of rocks. One mass of rock, more than twelve feet square, was thrown up out of the sea in a storm, not many years since, and now lies athwartwise, never to be moved unless another omnipotent wave shall give it another toss. On shore, such a rock would be a landmark for centuries. It is inconceivable how a sufficient mass of water could be brought to bear on this ponderous mass; but, not improbably, all the fragments piled upon one another round these islands have thus been flung to and fro at one time or another.

There is considerable land that would serve tolerably for pasture on Smutty Nose, and here and there a little enclosure of richer grass, built round with a strong stone wall. The same kind of enclosure is prevalent on Star Island,—each small proprietor fencing off his little bit of tillage or grass. Wild-flowers are abundant and various on these islands; the bayberry-bush is plentiful on Smutty Nose, and makes the hand that crushes it fragrant.

The hotel is kept by a Prussian, an old soldier, who fought at the Battle of Waterloo. We saw him in the barn,—a grey, heavy, round-skulled old fellow, troubled with deafness. The skipper of the wrecked sloop had, apparently, just been taking a drop of comfort, but still seemed downcast. He took passage in a fishing-vessel, the "Wave," of Kittery, for Portsmouth; and I know not why, but there was something that made me smile in his grim and gloomy look, his rusty, jammed hat, his rough and grisly beard, and in his mode of chewing tobacco, with much action of the jaws, getting out the juice as largely as possible, as men always do when disturbed in mind. I looked at him earnestly, and was conscious of something that marked him out from among the careless islanders around him. Being as much discomposed as it was possible for him to be, his feelings individualized the man and magnetized the observer. When he got aboard the fishing-vessel, he seemed not entirely at his ease, being accustomed to command and work amongst his own little crew, and now having nothing to do. Nevertheless, unconsciously perhaps, he lent a hand to whatever was going on, and yet had a kind of strangeness about him. As the "Wave" set sail, we were just starting in our dory, and a young fellow, an acquaintance of Mr. Thaxter, proposed to take us in tow; so we were dragged along at her stern very rapidly, and with a whitening wake, until we came off Hog Island. Then the dory was cast loose, and Mr. Thaxter rowed ashore against a head sea.

The day is still overcast, and the wind is from the eastward; but it does not increase, and the sun appears occasionally on the point of shining out. A boat—the "Fanny," I suppose, from Portsmouth—has just come to her moorings in front of the hotel. A sail-boat has put off from her, with a passenger in the stern. Pray God she bring me a letter with good news from home; for I begin to feel as if I had been long enough away.

There is a bowling-alley on Smutty Nose, at which some of the Star-Islanders were playing, when we were there. I saw only two dwelling-houses besides the hotel. Connected with Smutty Nose by a stone wall there is another little bit of island, called Malaga. Both are the property of Mr. Laighton.

Mr. Laighton says that the Spanish wreck occurred forty-seven years ago, instead of a hundred. Some of the dead bodies were found on Malaga, others on various parts of the next island. One or two had crept to a stone wall that traverses Smutty Nose, but were unable to get over it. One was found among the bushes the next summer. Mr. Haley had been buried at his own expense.

The skipper of the wrecked sloop, yesterday, was unwilling to go to Portsmouth until he was shaved,— his beard being of several days' growth. It seems to be the impulse of people under misfortune to put on their best clothes, and attend to the decencies of life.

The "Fanny" brought a passenger,—a thin, stiff, black-haired young man, who enters his name as Mr. Tufts, from Charlestown. He, and a country trader, his wife, sister, and two children (all of whom have been here several days), are now the only guests besides myself.

September 12*th*.—The night set in sullen and gloomy, and morning has dawned in pretty much the same way. The wind, however, seems rising somewhat, and grumbles past the angle of the house. Perhaps we shall see a storm yet from the eastward; and, having the whole sweep of the broad Atlantic between here and Ireland, I do not see why it should not be fully equal to a storm at sea.

It has been raining more or less all the forenoon, and now, at twelve o'clock, blows, as Mr. Laighton says, "half a gale" from the south-east. Through the opening of our shallow valley, towards the east, there is the prospect of a tumbling sea, with hundreds of white-caps chasing one another over it. In front of the hotel, being to leeward, the water near the shore is but slightly ruffled; but farther the sea is agitated, and the surf breaks over Square Rock. All round the horizon, landward as well as seaward, the view is shut in by a mist. Sometimes I have a dim sense of the continent beyond, but no more distinct than the thought of the other world to the unenlightened soul. The sheep bleat in their desolate pasture. The wind shakes the house. A loon, seeking, I suppose, some quieter resting-place than on the troubled waves, was seen swimming just now in the cove not more than a hundred yards from the hotel. Judging by the pother which this "half a gale" makes with the sea, it must have been a terrific time, indeed, when that great wave rushed and roared across the islands.

Since dinner, I have been to the eastern shore to look at the sea. It is a wild spectacle, but still, I suppose, lacks an infinite deal of being a storm. Outside of this island there is a long and low one (or two in a line), looking more like a reef of rocks than an island, and at the distance of a mile or more. There the surf and spray break gallantly,—white-sheeted forms rising up all at once, and hovering a moment in the air. Spots which, in calm times, are not discernible from the rest of the ocean, now are converted into white, foamy breakers. The swell of the waves against our shore makes a snowy depth, tinged with green, for many feet back from the shore. The longer waves swell, overtop, and rush upon the rocks; and, when they return, the waters pour back in a cascade. Against the outer points of Smutty Nose and Star Island there is a higher surf than here; because, the wind being from the south-east, these islands receive it first, and form a partial barrier in respect to this. While I looked, there was moisture in the air, and occasional spats of rain. The uneven places in the rocks were full of the fallen rain.

It is quite impossible to give an idea of these rocky shores, — how confusedly they are tossed together, lying in all directions; what solid ledges, what great fragments thrown out from the rest. Often the rocks are broken, square and angular, so as to form a kind of staircase; though, for the most part, such as would require a giant stride to ascend them.

Sometimes a black trap-rock runs through the bed of granite; sometimes the sea has eaten this away, leaving a long, irregular fissure. In some places, owing to the same cause, perhaps, there is a great hollow place excavated into the ledge, and forming a harbour into which the sea flows; and while there is foam and fury at the entrance, it is comparatively calm within. Some parts of the crag are as much as fifty feet of perpendicular height, down which you look over a bare and smooth descent, at the base of which is a shaggy margin of sea-weed. But it is vain to try to express this confusion. As much as anything else, it seems as if some of the massive materials of the world remained superfluous, after the Creator had finished, and were carelessly thrown down here, where the millionth part of them emerge from the sea, and in the course of thousands of years have become partially bestrewn with a little soil.

The wind has changed to south-west, and blows pretty freshly. The sun shone before it set; and the mist, which all day has overhung the land, now takes the aspect of a cloud,—drawing a thin veil between us and the shore, and rising above it. In our own atmosphere there is no fog nor mist.

September 13*th.*—I spent last evening, as well as part of the evening before, at Mr. Thaxter's. It is certainly a romantic incident to find such a young man on this lonely island; his marriage with the pretty Miranda is true romance. In our talk we have glanced over many matters, and, among the rest, that of the stage, to prepare himself for which was his first motive in coming hither. He appears quite to have given up any dreams of that kind now. What he will do on returning to the world, as his purpose is, I cannot imagine; but no doubt, through all their remaining life, both he and she will look back to this rocky ledge, with its handful of soil, as to a Paradise.

Last evening we (Mr., Mrs., and Miss Thaxter)

sat and talked of ghosts and kindred subjects; and they told me of the appearance of a little old woman in a striped gown, that had come into that house a few months ago. She was seen by nobody but an Irish nurse, who spoke to her, but received no answer. The little woman drew her chair up towards the fire, and stretched out her feet to warm them. By and by the nurse, who suspected nothing of her ghostly character, went to get a pail of water; and, when she came back, the little woman was not there. It being known precisely how many and what people were on the island, and that no such little woman was among them, the fact of her being a ghost is incontestable. I taught them how to discover the hidden sentiments of letters by suspending a gold ring over them. Ordinarily, since I have been here, we have spent the evening under the piazza, where Mr. Laighton sits to take the air. He seems to avoid the within-doors whenever he can. So there he sits in the sea-breezes, when inland people are probably drawing their chairs to the fireside; and there I sit with him,—not keeping up a continual flow of talk, but each speaking as any wisdom happens to come into his mind.

The wind, this morning, is from the north-westward, rather brisk, but not very strong. There is a scattering of clouds about the sky; but the atmosphere is singularly clear, and we can see several hills of the interior, the cloud-like White Mountains, and, along the shore, the long white beaches and the dotted dwellings, with great distinctness. Many small vessels spread their wings, and go seaward.

I have been rambling over the southern part of the island, and looking at the traces of habitations there. There are several enclosures,—the largest perhaps thirty yards square,—surrounded with a rough stone wall of very mossy antiquity, built originally broad and strong, two or three large stones in width, and piled up breast-high or more, and taking advantage of the extending ledge to make it higher. Within this enclosure there is almost a clear space of soil, which was formerly, no doubt, cultivated as a garden, but is now close cropt by the sheep and cattle, except where it produces thistles, or the poisonous weed called mercury, which seems to love these old walls, and to root itself in or near them. These walls are truly venerable, grey, and mossy; and you see at once that the hands that piled the stones must have been long ago turned to dust. Close by the enclosure is the hollow of an old cellar, with rocks tumbled into it, but the layers of stone at the side still to be traced, and bricks, broken or with rounded edges, scattered about, and perhaps pieces of lime; and weeds and grass growing about the whole. Several such sites of former human homes may be seen there, none of which can possibly be later than the Revolution, and probably they are as old as the settlement of the island. The site has Smutty Nose and Star opposite, with a road (that is, a water-road) between, varying from half-a-mile to a mile. Duck Island is also seen on the left; and, on the right, the shore of the mainland. Behind, the rising ground intercepts the view. Smith's monument is visible. I do not see where the inhabitants could have kept their boats, unless in the chasms worn by the sea into the rocks.

One of these chasms has a spring of fresh water in the gravelly base, down to which the sea has worn out. The chasm has perpendicular, though irregular, sides, which the waves have chiselled out very square. Its width varies from ten to twenty feet, widest towards the sea; and on the shelves, up and down the sides, some soil has been here and there accumulated, on which grow grass and wild-flowers,—such as golden-rod, now in bloom, and raspberry-bushes, the fruit of which I found ripe,—the whole making large parts of the sides of the chasm green, its verdure overhanging the strip of sea that dashes and foams into the hollow. Sea-weed, besides what grows upon and shags the submerged rocks, is tossed into the harbour, together with stray pieces of wood, chips, barrel-staves, or (as to-day) an entire barrel, or whatever else the sea happens to have on hand. The water rakes to and fro over the pebbles at the bottom of the chasm, drawing back, and leaving much of it bare, then rushing up, with more or less of foam and fury, according to the force and direction of the wind; though, owing to the protection of the adjacent islands, it can never have a gale blowing right into its mouth. The spring is situated so far down the chasm, that, at half or two-thirds tide, it is covered by the sea. Twenty minutes after the retiring of the tide suffices to restore to it its wonted freshness.

In another chasm, very much like the one here described, I saw a niche in the rock, about tall enough for a person of moderate stature to stand upright. It had a triangular floor and a top, and was just the place to hold the rudest statue that ever a savage made.

Many of the ledges on the island have yellow moss

or lichens spread on them in large patches. The moss of those stone walls does really look very old.

"Old Bab," the ghost, has a ring round his neck, and is supposed either to have been hung or to have had his throat cut, but he steadfastly declines telling the mode of his death. There is a luminous appearance about him as he walks, and his face is pale and very dreadful.

The "Fanny" arrived this forenoon, and sailed again before dinner. She brought, as passenger, a Mr. Balch, brother to the country trader who has been spending a few days here. On her return, she has swept the islands of all the non-residents except myself. The wind being ahead, and pretty strong, she will have to beat up, and the voyage will be anything but agreeable. The spray flew before her bows, and doubtless gave the passengers all a thorough wetting within the first half-hour.

The view of Star Island or Gosport from the north, is picturesque,—the village, or group of houses, being gathered pretty closely together in the centre of the island, with some green about them; and above all the other edifices, wholly displayed, stands the little stone church, with its tower and belfry. On the right is White Island, with the lighthouse; to the right of that, and a little to the northward, Londoner's Rock, where, perhaps, of old, some London ship was wrecked. To the left of Star Island, and nearer Hog, or Appledore, is Smutty Nose. Pour the blue sea about these islets, and let the surf whiten and steal up from their points, and from the reefs about them, (which latter whiten for an instant, and then are lost in the whelming and eddying depths,) the north-west wind the while raising thousands of whitecaps, and the evening sun shining solemnly over the expanse,—and it is a stern and lovely scene.

The valleys that intersect, or partially intersect, the island, are a remarkable feature. They appear to be of the same formation as the fissures in the rocks, but, as they extend farther from the sea, they accumulate a little soil along the irregular sides, and so become green and shagged with bushes, though with the rock everywhere thrusting itself through. The old people of the isles say that their fathers could remember when the sea, at high tide, flowed quite through the valley in which the hotel stands, and that boats used to pass. Afterwards it was a standing pond; then a morass, with cat-tail flags growing in it. It has filled up, so far as it is filled, by the soil being washed down from the higher ground on each side. The storms, meanwhile, have tossed up the shingle and paving-stones at each end of the valley, so as to form a barrier against the passage of any but such mighty waves as that which thundered through a year or two ago.

The old inhabitants lived in the centre or towards the south of the island, and avoided the north and east because the latter were so much bleaker in winter. They could moor their boats in the road, between Smutty Nose and Hog, but could not draw them up. Mr. Laighton found traces of old dwellings in the vicinity of the hotel, and it is supposed that the principal part of the population was on this island. I spent the evening at Mr. Thaxter's, and we drank a glass of his 1820 Schiedam. The northwest wind was high at ten o'clock, when I came home, the tide full, and the murmur of the waves broad and deep.

September 14*th*.—Another of the brightest of sunny mornings. The wind is not nearly so high as last night, but it is apparently still from the north-west, and serves to make the sea look very blue and cold. The atmosphere is so transparent that objects seem perfectly distinct along the mainland. To-day

I must be in Portsmouth; to-morrow, at home. A brisk west or north-west wind, making the sea so blue, gives a very distinct outline in its junction with the sky.

September 16*th*.—On Tuesday, the 14th, there was no opportunity to get to the mainland. Yesterday morning opened with a south-east rain, which continued all day. The "Fanny" arrived in the forenoon, with some coal for Mr. Laighton, and sailed again before dinner, taking two of the maids of the house; but as it rained pouring, and as I could not, at any rate, have got home to-night, there would have been no sense in my going. It began to clear up in the decline of the day; the sun shot forth some golden arrows a little before his setting; and the sky was perfectly clear when I went to bed, after spending the evening at Mr. Thaxter's. This morning is clear and bright; but the wind is north-west, making the sea look blue and cold, with little breaks of white foam. It is unfavourable for a trip to the mainland; but doubtless I shall find an opportunity of getting ashore before night.

The highest part of Appledore is about eighty feet above the sea. Mr. Laighton has seen whales off the island,—both on the eastern side and between it and the mainland; once a great crowd of them, as many as fifty. They were drawn in by pursuing their food,—a small fish called herring-bait, which came ashore in such abundance that Mr. Laighton dipped up baskets full of them. No attempt was made to take the whales.

There are vague traditions of trees on these islands. One of them, Cedar Island, is said to have been named from the trees that grew on it. The matter appears improbable, though, Mr. Thaxter says, large quantities of soil are annually washed into the sea; so that the islands may have been better clad with earth and its productions than now.

Mrs. Thaxter tells me that there are several burial-places on this island; but nobody has been buried here since the Revolution. Her own marriage was the first one since that epoch, and her little Karl, now three months old, the first-born child in all those eighty years.

[*Then follow extracts from the Church Records of Gosport.*]

This book of the Church records of Gosport is a small folio, well bound in dark calf, and about an inch thick; the paper very stout, with a water-mark of an armed man in a sitting posture, holding a spear. . . . over a lion, who brandishes a sword; on alternate pages the crown, and beneath it the letters G. R. The motto of the former device Pro Patria. The book is written in a very legible hand, probably by the Rev. Mr. Tucke. The ink is not much faded.

Concord, March 9th, 1853.—Finished, this day, the last story of "Tanglewood Tales." They were written in the following order:—
 " The Pomegranate Seeds."
 " The Minotaur."
 " The Golden Fleece."
 " The Dragons' Teeth."
 " Circe's Palace."
 " The Pygmies."

The introduction is yet to be written. Wrote it 13th March. I went to Washington (my first visit) on 14th April.

Caresses, expressions of one sort or another, are necessary to the life of the affections, as leaves are to the life of a tree. If they are wholly restrained love will die at the roots.

June 9th.—Cleaning the attic to-day, here at the Wayside, the woman found an immense snake, flat and outrageously fierce, thrusting out its tongue. Ellen, the cook, killed it. She called it an adder, but it appears to have been a striped snake. It seems a fiend, haunting the house. On further inquiry, the snake is described as plaided with brown and black.

Cupid in these latter times has probably laid aside his bow and arrows, and uses fire-arms,—a pistol,—perhaps a revolver.

I burned great heaps of old letters and other papers, a little while ago, preparatory to going to England. Among them were hundreds of ———'s letters. The world has no more such, and now they are all dust and ashes. What a trustful guardian of secret matters is fire! What should we do without fire and death?

THE END.

London: Printed by SMITH, ELDER & Co., Old Bailey, E.C.

www.ingramcontent.com/pod-product-compliance
Lightning Source LLC
Chambersburg PA
CBHW022028240426
43667CB00042B/1225